Madame Alexander

Collector's Dolls Price Guide #23

Linda C. Crowsey

COLLECTOR BOOKS

A Division of Schroeder Publishing Co., Inc.

Searching For A Publisher?

We are always looking for knowledgeable people considered to be experts within their fields. If you feel that there is a real need for a book on your collectible subject and have a large comprehensive collection contact Collector Books.

On the cover:
Left: Hard plastic — 8", 1956 Wendy wears a charming ensemble.
Top right: Cloth 1930's Little Shaver.
Bottom right: 9" composition McGuffey Ana.

Cover design: Beth Summers
Book design: Kent Henry

Founder: Patricia R. Smith

Additional copies of this book may be ordered from:

Collector Books
P.O. Box 3009
Paducah, Kentucky 42002-3009

@ $9.95. Add $2.00 for postage and handling.

Dedication ...

Madame Alexander Collector's Dolls Price Guide #23 *is dedicated to Madame Beatrice Alexander and the Alexander Doll Company for giving Collectors 75 years of the finest quality dolls that are treasured all over the world. Madame Alexander devoted her life to making beautiful dolls that bring endless joy to children and adults. With her dolls of fashion, movies, paintings, books, and beautiful babies, Madame Alexander has set a standard of the finest quality that will live on forever.*

— Linda C. Crowsey

— Madame Alexander Doll Club —

For membership information write to:
Madame Alexander Doll Club (M.A.D.C.)
P.O. Box 330
Mundelein, IL 60060-0330

PHOTO CREDITS

Gary Green, Susan Huey, Nancy and Kathleen LaBounty, Lahanta McIntyre, Chris McWilliams, Flip and Florence Phelps, Lillian Roth, Dwight Smith, Helen Thomas, Turn of Century Antiques, Susan York.

— Seventy-Five Years of Madame Alexander Dolls —
1923 – 1998

Madame Beatrice Alexander was born on March 9, 1895, in New York City. Her father, Maurice Alexander, owned a doll hospital where dolls were repaired and new dolls sold. Beatrice and her three sisters grew up seeing the joy these dolls brought to children. Madame married Phillip Behrman in 1912. Their only child, Mildred, was born in 1915. Madame and her sisters made the first dolls of cloth with painted faces. With the success of the cloth dolls, Madame joined with her husband to form the Alexander Doll Company in 1923. This Price Guide lists the award-winning dolls that the Alexander Doll Company has made in cloth, composition, hard plastic, vinyl, and porcelain.

I purchased my first Madame Alexander doll, Renoir, for my daughter Susan's Christmas present in 1975. I joined the Madame Alexander Doll Club in 1976 and met Madame Alexander in person at Disney World in 1983. Madame and I corresponded regularly. It was a great thrill for me when Susan met Madame at the 1987 Madame Alexander Doll Convention. My sincere thanks to the Alexander Doll Company for the 1997 tour of the factory and the Fifth Avenue showroom in New York City. It was a dream come true to be where Madame created and the Alexander Doll Company continues to create the most beautiful dolls in the world. Madame Beatrice Alexander died in 1990 and I miss her, but she will not be forgotten. Her beautiful creations live on cherished by collectors.

Madame Alexander and Susan Crowsey in 1987.

What is a Price Guide?

Price guides must be based upon values for a perfect doll since all collectors need accurate prices for insurance purposes. Insurance companies and postal services must have a way to determine the value of a damaged or stolen doll. Collectors must also have a way to appraise and insure their collection. A price guide, while not the final word, is a starting point to determine the value of a doll. The prices listed are for perfect dolls. Imperfect dolls will bring considerably less than an exceptional doll, which collectors call "tissue mint."

TURKEY (left) with perfect hair and coloring. A mint doll. TURKEY (right) with little cheek coloring, stringy hair, faded clothes, shelf worn.

PERFECT DOLLS
- Complete outfit on correct doll
- Beautiful face color
- Clothes and doll in excellent condition
- Has all accessories, such as hats, etc.
- Clothes not laundered or ironed
- Hair in original set

LESS THAN PERFECT DOLLS
- Re-dressed or has part of original clothes
- Washed, cleaned, ironed clothes
- Stains, soil, faded, shelf dust
- Faded face color
- Tag cut or missing
- Hair mussed or dirty

EXCEPTIONAL DOLLS
- Extremely rare doll
- Has wrist tag or original box
- Autographed by Madame Alexander
- Unique outfit or doll
- "Tissue Mint" condition
- Has wardrobe or trunk
- Matched set of same year (such as *Little Women*)

There is no guarantee that any doll, antique or modern, will appreciate year after year. Prices remain high on exceptional dolls and always will.

Original boxes are important for the information on the box is valuable in determining the age and manufacturer of the doll. Boxes can be a fire hazard. It is possible to fold most boxes and store them inside a larger box and place the boxes in an airy dry room. Collectors will pay a higher price for a doll in its original box. Beware of storing dolls for a long time in their boxes — clothing, wigs, and vinyl can fade or change colors. Also, vinyl dolls tend to become greasy or sticky when stored in their boxes.

MOLD MARKS

Mold marks can be the same for an extended period of time. For example, 14" "Mary Ann" dolls will be marked "1965" which is the first year the doll was made. From then to now all "Mary Ann" dolls will be marked "1965." Another example is the 21" "Jacqueline" first introduced in 1961. This doll has been used for the Portraits since 1965 and up to now still bears the 1961 date mark on head. Determining the exact year can be difficult for that reason.

Doll Names

The dolls named after real people are listed with last name first. (Example: "Bliss, Betty Taylor.") Make-believe doll names will be listed with first name first. (Example: "Tommy Snooks.")

Box Numbers

Order/box numbers for the 8" dolls with "0" prefix (example 0742) were used in 1973 only. It must be noted the box numbers found with doll's name are from the Madame Alexander catalogs, but many dolls were placed in wrong boxes by the stores from which they were sold.

Abbreviations

h.p. – hard plastic
compo. – composition
FAD – factory altered dress
SLNW – straight leg, non-walker
SLW – straight leg walker
BKW – bend knee walker
BK – bend knee

U.F.D.C. – United Federation of Doll Clubs
M.A.D.C. – Madame Alexander Doll Club
C.U. – Collectors United

Auction Prices

Auction prices bear little or no effect on general pricing for Madame Alexander dolls. Recently, several dolls were sold at auction for exorbitant prices. It is as simple as two or more people wanting the same item — the bidders just get carried away! Another reason is the rarity or the pristine mint condition of a doll. This type of doll is *extremely* difficult to find and warrants the high auction price.

The final word is Madame Alexander dolls have always been collectible and should continue to be. They should endure in time and value. Wise collectors purchase dolls that they really like rather than purchasing dolls that are rumored to go up in value. Then, even if the doll's value doesn't go up, the collector has a beautiful doll that he or she loves. We hope you will continue to build the collections you desire, be they of older dolls or the wonderful current dolls that become available each year.

THE MANY FACES OF MADAME ALEXANDER DOLLS

WENDY ANN (Composition)

TINY & LITTLE BETTY

PRINCESS ELIZABETH

MAGGIE

MARGARET (O'BRIEN)

CISSY

THE MANY FACES OF MADAME ALEXANDER DOLLS

ELISE (1950s – 1960s)

LISSY (1950s)

CISSETTE

MARY-BEL

JACQUELINE

MARY ANN

THE MANY FACES OF MADAME ALEXANDER DOLLS

ELISE (1960s – 1980s)

POLLY & LESLIE

NANCY DREW

WENDY ANN — New 1988 Face

MAGGIE MIXUP (1960 – 1961)

WENDY ANN (1953 – 1965)

Please read "What is a Price Guide?" for additional information.

ACTIVE MISS — 18" h.p., 1954 only, (Violet/Cissy) 850.00
ADAMS, ABIGAIL — 1976–1978, Presidents' Ladies/First Ladies Series, First Set (Mary Ann) 115.00
ADAMS, LOUISA — 1976–1978, Presidents' Ladies/First Ladies Series, First Set (Louisa). 115.00
ADDAMS FAMILY — #31130, 1997, set 4 dolls (8", 10") and Thing. 350.00
    #31110, 1997, 10" Gomez and Morticia 180.00
    #31120, 1997, 8" Wednesday and Pugsley 160.00
AFRICA — 8" h.p., #766, 1966–1971, BK (Wendy Ann) 285.00
    8" h.p. straight leg, re-issued, #523–583, 1988–1992, (Wendy Ann) 50.00
AGATHA — 18" h.p. (Cissy)
    1954 only, Me and My Shadow Series, rose taffeta dress, excellent face color 1,850.00
    8" h.p. (Wendy Ann), #00308, 1953–1954, black top and floral gown . . . . 1,250.00 up
    21" Portrait, #2171, 1967, red gown (Jacqueline) 650.00
        #2297, 1974, rose gown with full length cape (Jacqueline) 450.00
        #2291, 1975, blue with white sequin trim (Jacqueline) 375.00
        #2294, 1976, blue with white rick-rack trim (Jacqueline) 350.00
        #2230, 1979, 1980, lavender 300.00
        #2230, 1981, turquoise blue (Jacqueline) 275.00
    10" Portrette, #1171, 1968 only, red velvet (Cissette) 425.00
AGNES — Cloth/felt, 1930's. 750.00
ALADDIN — 8" h.p., #482, 1993; #140482, 1994 only, Storybook Series 55.00
ALASKA — 8", #302, 1990–1992, Americana Series (Maggie smile face) 55.00
ALBANIA — 8" straight leg, #526, 1987 only (Wendy Ann). 60.00
ALCOTT, LOUISA MAY — 14", #1529, 1989–1990, Classic Series (Mary Ann) 85.00
    8" h.p., #409, 1992 only, Storyland Series (Wendy Ann). 65.00
ALEGRIA — 10", h.p., #20118, 1996 Cirque du Soleil, silver outfit. 95.00
ALEXANDER RAG TIME DOLLS — Cloth, 1938–1939 only. . . . . 850.00 up
ALEXANDER-KINS — 7½–8" h.p., must have excellent face color
  (Also referred to as WENDY, WENDY ANN, or WENDY-KIN.) *If doll is not listed here, see regular listing for name.*
  (Add more for mint or mint in box dolls. Special hairdos are higher priced.)
    Straight leg non-walker, 1953 (Add more for Quiz-Kins)   **Mint**
      Coat/hat (dress) 550.00

8" "Wendy in Organdy Dress,"
1965, #621. Tag: Wendykin.

8" Wendy from the early 1960's. Tag:
Madame Alexander, New York, All Rights
Reserved. Lime checked cotton pants.

8" WENDY GOES ICE SKATING. Bend knee walker.

"Mother, My I Go Out to Play," 1957, #374. Bend knee walker. Wool jacket, velvet pants.

ALEXANDER-KINS, CONTINUED . . .

Cotton dress/organdy pinafore/hat 550.00
Cotton dress/cotton pinafore/hat. 500.00
Dresser/doll/wardrobe, mint . . . . 3,000.00 up
Easter doll . . . . 925.00 up
Felt jackets/pleated skirt dresses 550.00
Garden Party long gown . . . . 1,250.00 up
Jumper/one-piece bodysuit 350.00
Nightgown. 300.00
Nude/perfect doll (excellent face color) 275.00
Organdy dress/cotton pinafore/hat 525.00
Organdy dress/organdy pinafore/hat 550.00
Satin dress/cotton pinafore/hat 600.00
Satin dress/organdy pinafore/hat 600.00
Sleeveless satin dress/organdy or cotton pinafore 475.00
Taffeta dress/cotton pinafore/hat 600.00
Robe/nightgown or P.J.'s 350.00
Straight leg walker, 1954-1955, must have good face color. (Add more for mint or mint in box dolls.)
Basic doll in box/panties/shoes/socks. 400.00
Coat/hat (dress) . . . . 375.00 up
Cotton dress/pinafore/hat. . . . . 375.00 up
Cotton school dress 325.00
Day in Country 850.00
Garden Party long gown . . . . 1,200.00 up
Maypole Dance 550.00
Nightgown, robe, or PJs 200.00
Jumper dress with blouse effect, any material. 350.00
Organdy party dress/hat. . . . . 450.00 up
Riding Habit . . . . 350.00 up
Sailor dress. . . . . 850.00 up

ALEXANDER-KINS, CONTINUED . . .

Sleeveless organdy dress	325.00
Swimsuits (mint)	295.00
Taffeta/satin party dress/hat	475.00 up

Bend knee walker, 1956–1965, must have good face color. (Add more for mint or mint in box dolls.)
"Alexander-kin" dropped in 1963 and "Wendy Ann" used through 1965

Nude (Excellent face color)	125.00
Basic doll in box/panties/shoes/socks (mint in box)	325.00
Carcoat set	725.00
Cherry Twin	Each – 1,500.00 up
Coat/hat/dress	325.00
Cotton dress/cotton pinafore/hat	350.00
Cotton or satin dress/organdy pinafore/hat	375.00 up
Easter Egg/doll, 1965, 1966 only	1,400.00 up
Felt jacket/pleated skirt/dress/cap or hat	375.00
Felt jacket/skirt/dress/cap/hat, 1965	475.00 up
First Dancing Dress (gown)	725.00
Flowergirl	850.00 up
French braid/cotton dress, 1965	550.00
June Wedding	750.00
Long party dress	750.00 up
Nightgown/robe	175.00
NEIMAN-MARCUS (clothes must be on correct doll with correct hairdo)	
Doll in case with all clothes	1,350.00 up
Name of store printed on dress material	700.00
2 pc. playsuit, navy with red trim	450.00
Robe, navy	325.00
Nude, perfect doll with excellent face color, bend knee/non-walker	85.00
Organdy dress/hat, 1965	325.00
Organdy dress/organdy pinafore/hat	375.00
Riding habit, boy or girl	475.00
Devon Horse Show	725.00
Riding habit, check pants, girl, 1965	375.00
Riding habit, check pants, boy, 1965	375.00
Sewing Kit/doll, 1965, 1966 only	950.00 up
Skater	525.00
Sleeveless school dress	275.00
Sundress	300.00
Swimsuits, beach outfits	300.00
Taffeta party dress/hat	450.00
Tennis	400.00

ALGERIA — 8", straight leg, #528, 1987–1988 only (Maggie) 55.00

ALICE — 18" h.p., 1951 only, saran wig to waist (Maggie) 750.00

ALICE AND HER PARTY KIT — 1965 only, included case, wardrobe and wigs, mint (Mary Ann) 750.00

ALICE (IN WONDERLAND) —

16" cloth, 1930 flat face, eyes painted to side	875.00
1933 formed mask face	675.00
7" compo., 1930's (Tiny Betty)	325.00
9" compo., 1930's (Little Betty)	350.00
11–14" compo., 1936–1940 (Wendy Ann)	400.00–450.00
13" compo., 1930's, has swivel waist (Wendy Ann)	425.00
14½–18" compo., 1948–1949 (Margaret)	475.00–725.00
21" compo., 1948–1949 (Margaret, Wendy Ann)	950.00
14" h.p., 1950 (Maggie)	650.00
17–23" h.p. 1949–1950 (Maggie & Margaret)	625.00–800.00 up
15", 18", 23" h.p., 1951–1952 (Maggie & Margaret)	500.00–800.00 up

ALICE (IN WONDERLAND), CONTINUED . . .

14" h.p. with trousseau, 1951–1952 (Maggie)	1,600.00 up
15" h.p., 1951–1952 (Maggie & Margaret)	575.00
17" h.p., 1949–1950 (Maggie & Margaret)	600.00
23" h.p., 1942–1952 (Maggie & Margaret)	875.00 up
29" cloth/vinyl, 1952 (Barbara Jane)	700.00 up
8" h.p., #465–#590, 1955–1956 (Wendy Ann)	750.00 up
8", #494, Storyland Series, blue/white eyelet pinafore 1990–1992	60.00
#492, 1993, #140492, 1994 blue/white with red trim	60.00
8" h.p., 1972–1976, Disney crest colors, (Disneyland, Disney World)	450.00
8" h.p., blue with lace trim, organdy pinafore, 1995	60.00
8" h.p. #13000, 1997, Alice with calendar, blue party dress, gold crown	75.00
12", Prom Party set, 1963 (Lissy)	950.00
14" plastic/vinyl, #1452 to 1974, #1552, 1966–1992, Literature & Classic Series (Mary Ann)	90.00
14" plastic/vinyl, #87001, 1996 Storyland Friends	110.00
10", 1991, with white rabbit (see Disney under Special Events/Exclusives)	375.00
18", #16001, 1996 Rag Doll Series (cloth doll)	50.00
ALL STAR — 8" h.p., #346–346-1, Americana Series, 1993 white or black, 1994 white only	65.00
ALLISON — 18" cloth/vinyl, 1990–1991	110.00
ALPINE BOY AND GIRL — 1992 (see Christmas Shoppe under Special Events/Exclusives)	185.00 pair
ALTAR BOY — 8" h.p., #311, 1991 only, Americana Series	65.00
AMANDA — 8" h.p., #489, 1961 only, Americana Series, burnt orange/lace trim (Wendy Ann)	1,900.00 up
AMERICAN BABIES — 16–18" cloth, 1930's	175.00–350.00
AMERICAN BEAUTY — 10" Portrette, #1142, 1991–1992, all pink	85.00
AMERICAN FARM COUPLE — 8", 1997, #22160, 1930's rural America	130.00
AMERICAN GIRL — 7–8" compo., 1938 (Tiny Betty)	325.00
9–11" compo., 1937 (Little Betty, Wendy Ann)	350.00–450.00
8" h.p., #388, #788, 1962–1963, became "McGuffey Ana" in 1964–1965 (Wendy Ann)	375.00
AMERICAN INDIAN — 9" compo., 1938–1939 (Little Betty)	350.00
AMERICAN TOTS — 16–21" cloth, dressed in child's fashions	275.00–500.00
AMERICAN WOMEN'S VOLUNTEER SERVICE (A.W.V.S.) — 14" compo., 1942 (Wendy Ann)	825.00 up
AMISH BOY — 8" h.p., BK, #727, 1966–1969, Americana Series (Wendy Ann)	350.00
AMISH GIRL — 8" h.p. BK, #726, 1966–1969, Americana Series (Wendy Ann)	375.00
AMY — (see Little Women)	
AMY GOES TO PARIS TRUNK SET — 8", #14635, 1996	180.00
AMY THE BRIDE — 10", #14622, 1996, ivory lace dress	95.00
ANASTASIA — 10" Portrette, #1125, 1988–1989 (Cissette)	85.00
14" (see M.A.D.C. under Special Events/Exclusives)	225.00
ANATOLIA — 8", straight leg, #524, 1987 only	65.00
ANGEL AND 8" MUSIC BOX CRECHE — 8", #19530, 1997, Nativity set	250.00
ANGEL — 8", in pink, blue, off-white gowns (Wendy & Maggie)	900.00 up
BABY ANGEL — 8" h.p. #480, 1955, multi-layered chiffon wings (Wendy Ann)	900.00 up
GUARDIAN ANGEL — 8", #480, 1954 only, (Wendy Ann)	825.00 up
GUARDIAN ANGEL — 8", #618, 1961 (Maggie smile face)	750.00
GUARDIAN ANGEL — 10", #10602, 1995, first in series, all pink with white wings	110.00
PRISTINE ANGEL — 10", #10604, 1995, second in series, white with gold trim	110.00
ANGEL FACE — (see Shirley's Doll House under Special Events/Exclusives)	125.00
ANGEL TREE TOPPER — (see Tree Topper)	
ANNA AND THE KING OF SIAM — 8", 1996, #14656, sold as set	160.00
ANNA BALLERINA — 18" compo., 1940, Pavlova (Wendy Ann)	950.00 up
ANNABELLE — 14–15" h.p., 1951–1952 only, Kate Smith's stories of Annabelle (Maggie)	575.00
14–15" trousseau/trunk, 1952 only, FAO Schwarz (Maggie)	1,500.00 up
18" h.p., 1951–1952 (Maggie)	675.00
20–23" h.p., 1951–1952 (Maggie)	700.00–875.00 up
ANNABELLE AT CHRISTMAS — (see Belks & Leggett under Special Events/Exclusives)	95.00 up

ANNA KARENINA — 21" Portrait, #2265, 1991 (Jacqueline) 350.00
ANNE OF GREEN GABLES — 14", #1530, 1989–1990 only (Mary Ann) 140.00
   14", #1579, 1992–1994, Goes to School, with trunk/wardrobe (Louisa/Jennifer) 250.00
   14", #1570 in 1993 only, #261501 in 1995, Arrives at Station 165.00
   14", 1993, Becomes the Teacher 125.00
   8" h.p. 1994–1995, #260417, At the Station (Wendy Ann) 85.00
   8" h.p. 1994, #260418 puff sleeve dress 75.00
   8" h.p., #26423, 1995, concert dress 75.00
   8" h.p., #26421, 1995, trunk playset 195.00
ANNETTE — 1993 (see Disney under Special Events/Exclusives) 475.00
ANNIE THE ARTIST — 20", #35001, 1996, artist outfit, crayons 125.00
ANNIE LAURIE — 14" compo., 1937 (Wendy Ann) 650.00
   17" compo., 1937 (Wendy Ann) 925.00
ANTOINETTE — 21" compo., 1946, extra makeup, must be mint (Wendy Ann) . . . . 2,100.00 up
ANTOINETTE, MARIE — 21", 1987–1988 only, multi-floral with pink front insert (Wendy Ann) 425.00
ANTONY, MARK — 12", #1310, 1980–1985, Portraits of History (Nancy Drew) 75.00
APPLE ANNIE OF BROADWAY — 8" h.p., 1953–1954 (Wendy Ann) . . . . 1,000.00 up
APPLE PIE — 14", #1542, 1991 only, Doll Classics (Mary Ann) 95.00
APRIL — 14", #1533, 1990–1991, Doll Classics (Mary Ann & Jennifer) 95.00
ARGENTINE BOY — 8" h.p., BKW & BK, #772, 1965 only (Wendy Ann) 550.00
ARGENTINE GIRL — 8" h.p., BK, #0771-571, 1965–1972 (Wendy Ann) 150.00
   BKW, #771 (Wendy Ann) 195.00
   8" h.p., straight legs, #571, 1973–1976, marked "Alex" 65.00
   8" h.p., straight legs, #571, 1976–1986 (1985–1986 white face) 50.00
ARMENIA — 8", #507, 1989–1990 (Wendy Ann) 65.00
ARRIVING IN AMERICA — 8" h.p., #326, 1992–1993 only, Americana Series (Wendy Ann) 75.00
ARTIE — 12" plastic/vinyl, 1962, sold through FAO Schwarz (Smarty) 285.00
ASHLEY — 8", #628, 1990 only, Scarlett Series, tan jacket/hat 90.00
   8" h.p., #633, 1991–1992 only, Scarlett Series, as Confederate officer 90.00
ASTOR — 9" early vinyl toddler, 1953 only, gold organdy dress & bonnet 150.00
ASTROLOGICAL MONTH DOLLS — 14–17" compo., 1938 (Wendy) 525.00
AUNT AGATHA — 8" h.p., #434, 1957 (Wendy Ann) . . . . 1,100.00 up
AUNT BETSY — Cloth/felt, 1930's 900.00
AUNT MARCH — 8", #14621, 1996 . . . . 65.00
AUNT PITTY PAT — 14–17" compo., 1939 (Wendy Ann) from "Gone with the Wind" . . . . 1,500.00 up
   8" h.p., #435, 1957 (Wendy Ann) from "Gone with the Wind" . . . . 1,650.00 up
   8" h.p., straight leg, #636, 1991–1992, Scarlett Series 95.00
AUNTIE EM — 8" h.p., #14515, 1995 only, Wizard of Oz series 70.00
AUSTRALIA — 8", #504, 1990–1991 only (Wendy Ann) 55.00
AUSTRIA BOY * — 8" h.p., 1974–1989 (Wendy Ann)
   Straight legs, #599–#533, 1973–1975, marked "Alex" 70.00
   #599, 1976–1989, marked "Alexander" (1985–1987 white face) 50.00
AUSTRIA GIRL * — 8" h.p., 1974–1993 (Wendy Ann)
     Straight legs, #598, 1973–1975, marked "Alex." 75.00
     #598–#532, 1976–1990, marked "Alexander" (1985–1987 white face) 50.00
     Reintroduced #110539 (Maggie), 1994 only 65.00
AUTUMN — 14", 1993, Changing Seasons Doll with four outfits 150.00
AUTUMN IN N.Y. — (see First Modern Doll Club under Special Events/Exclusives) 175.00
AUTUMN LEAVES — 14", 1994, Classic Dolls 135.00
AVRIL, JANE — 10" (see Marshall Fields under Special Events/Exclusives) 150.00

* FORMERLY TYROLEAN BOY AND GIRL

Please read "What is a Price Guide?" for additional information.

BABBIE — Cloth with long thin legs, inspired by Katharine Hepburn . . . . 1,000.00 up
    16", cloth child doll, 1934–1936 . . . . 775.00 up
    14" h.p. (Maggie) . . . . 800.00 up
BABETTE — 10" Portrette, #1117, 1988–1989, black short dress (Cissette) 85.00
BABS — 20" h.p., 1949 (Maggie) 850.00
BABS SKATER — 18" compo. (Margaret) . . . . 1,200.00 up
    15" h.p., 1948–1950 (Margaret) . . . . 1,000.00 up
    17–18" h.p. . . . . 1,200.00 up
    21" h.p. . . . . 1,300.00 up
BABSIE BABY — Compo./cloth, moving tongue 550.00
BABSIE SKATER (ROLLER) — 15", 1941 (Princess Elizabeth) . . . . 750.00 up
BABY BETTY — 10–12" compo., 1935–1936 . . . . 275.00
BABY BROTHER AND SISTER — 20", cloth/vinyl, 1977–1979 (Mary Mine) . . . . 100.00 each
    14", 1979–1982 . . . . 85.00 each
    14", re-introduced 1989 only . . . . 75.00 each
BABY CLOWN — See Clowns
BABY ELLEN — 14", 1965–1972 (black Sweet Tears) 125.00
BABY GENIUS — 11" all cloth, 1930's 425.00
    11–12" compo./cloth, 1930's–1940's . . . . 225.00 up
    16" compo./cloth, 1930's–1940's 225.00
    22", compo./cloth, 1940's 550.00
    15", 18", h.p. head, vinyl limbs, 1949–1950 (some get sticky or turn dark) 100.00–150.00
    21" h.p. head, vinyl limbs, 1952–1955 . . . . 350.00
    8" h.p./vinyl, 1956–1962 (see Little Genius)
BABY JANE — 16" compo., 1935 . . . . 950.00 up
BABY LYNN — 20" cloth/vinyl, 1973–1976 . . . . 135.00
    14" cloth/vinyl, 1973–1976 . . . . 125.00

8" "BEST MAN," 1955, #461. Straight leg walker. Hard plastic.

BABY McGuffey — 22–24" compo., 1937 . . . . 275.00

    20" cloth/vinyl, 1971–1976 . . . . 190.00

    14" cloth/vinyl, 1972–1978 . . . . 150.00

BABY PRECIOUS — 14" cloth/vinyl, 1975 only 95.00

    21" cloth/vinyl, 1974–1976 . . . . 135.00

BABY IN LOUIS VUITTON TRUNK/WARDROBE OR WICKER BASKET WITH LEGS — Any year . . . . 900.00 up

BABY SHAVER — 12", cloth h.p., 1941–1943, yellow floss wig, round painted eyes (Little Shaver) . . . . . 650.00 up

BAD LITTLE GIRL — 16" cloth, 1966 only, blue dress, eyes and mouth turned down, looking sad 250.00

BALI — 8" h.p., #533, 1993 only 60.00

BALLERINA — (Also see individual dolls – Leslie, Margaret, etc.)

    9" compo., 1935–1941 (Little Betty) 350.00

    11–13", 1930's (Betty) 400.00

    11–14" compo., 1936–1938 (Wendy Ann) 425.00

    17" compo., 1938–1941 (Wendy Ann) . . . . 600.00 up

    21" compo., 1947, "Debra" ("Deborah") Portrait ballerina in mint condition (Wendy Ann) . . . . . . 3,200.00 up

    8" h.p., must have excellent face color. (Wendy Ann)

        (Also see Enchanted Doll House under Special Events/Exclusives) 125.00

        (Also see M.A.D.C. under Special Events/Exclusives) 250.00

        SLNW, #354, 1953–1954, lavender, yellow, or pink . . . . 750.00 up

            8" straight leg, #0730, #530, #430, 1973–1992 (1985–1987 white face) 85.00

        SLW, #454, 1955, lavender, yellow, pink, or white . . . . 650.00 up

        BKW, #564, 1954–1960, golden yellow 550.00

            #454, 1955, white 500.00

            #564, 1956, rose 600.00

            #564–631, 1956, yellow 650.00

            #364, 1957, blue 425.00

            #544, 1958, pink 375.00

            #420, 1959, gold 700.00

            #420, 1961, lavender 725.00

            #640, 1964, pink 550.00

    BK, #620-730, 1965–1972, yellow 375.00

**18" ELISE BRIDE, 1963, "Marybel" face. Mint,
in original box.**

BALLERINA, CONTINUED . . .

    #440-730, 1962–1972, blue 250.00

    #440-730, 1962–1972, pink 225.00

    SLNW, #330, 1990–1991 (black or white dolls, 1991), Americana Series, white/gold outfit (Wendy Ann) 75.00

    #331–331-1, 1992, black or white doll in pink/silver outfit (Wendy Ann) 60.00

    #331, 1993, white doll only pink/silver outfit 55.00

    #100331, 1994-1995, white doll, pink tutu 60.00

    10–11" h.p., 1957–1959, must have excellent face color (Cissette) 375.00

    12", 1964 only (Janie) 300.00

    12", 1989–1990, "Muffin," (Janie) 85.00

    12", 1990–1992 only, Romance Collection (Nancy Drew) 85.00

    12", 1993 only, in lavender (Lissy) 110.00

    14", 1963 only (Melinda) . . . . 325.00 up

    15–18" h.p., 1950–1952, must have good face color (Margaret) 625.00–650.00

    16½" h.p., 1957–1964 jointed ankles, knees & elbows, must have good face color (Elise) 375.00

        1957, yellow, rare 850.00

        1958, white 350.00

        1959, gold 350.00

        1960, pink 350.00

        1961, upswept hairdo, pink 400.00

        1962, blue 350.00

        1963–1964 only, small flowers in 1963; large flowers in 1964 (Marybel) (18" also Elise) 400.00

    17" plastic/vinyl, 1967–1989, discontinued costume (Elise) 150.00

    17" plastic/vinyl, 1990–1991, "Firebird" and "Swan Lake" (Elise) 150.00

    17", 1966–1971 only (Leslie - black doll) 350.00

BARBARA JANE — 29" cloth/vinyl, 1952 only, mint 500.00

BARBARA LEE — 8", 1955, name given by FAO Schwarz 650.00

BARBARY COAST — 10" h.p., 1962–1963, Portrette (Cissette) . . . . 1,500.00 up

BARTON, CLARA — 10", #1130, 1989 only, Portrette, wears nurse's outfit (Cissette) 95.00

BASEBALL BOY — 8", #16313, 1997, red, white baseball outfit 58.00

BASEBALL GIRL — 8", #16300, baseball outfit with ball glove 58.00

BATHING BEAUTY — (see U.F.D.C. under Special Events/Exclusives) 275.00

BEAST — 12", 1992 only, Romance Series (Nancy Drew) 100.00

    8" #140487 Storyland Series - 1994, Fairy Tales Series - 1995 . . . . 70.00

BEAU BRUMMEL — Cloth, 1930s 750.00

BEAUTY — 12", 1992 only, Romance Series (Nancy Drew) 95.00

    8" #140486 Storyland Series - 1994, Fairy Tales Series - 1995 . . . . 80.00

BEAUTY QUEEN — 10" h.p., 1961 only (Cissette) 295.00

BEAUX ARTS DOLLS — 18" h.p., 1953 only (Margaret, Maggie) . . . . 2,000.00 up

BEDDY-BYE BROOKE — (see FAO Schwarz under Special Events/Exclusives) 125.00

BEDDY-BYE BRENDA (Brooke's sister) (see FAO Schwarz under Special Events/Exclusives) . . . . 200.00 set

BEING A PROM QUEEN — (see Wendy Loves)

BEING JUST LIKE MOMMY — (See Wendy Loves)

BELGIUM — 8" h.p., BK, #762, 1972 only (Wendy Ann) 125.00

    8" straight legs, #0762, #562, 1973–1975, marked "Alex" 75.00

    8" straight legs, #562, 1976–1988, marked "Alexander" (1985–1987 white face) 60.00

    7" compo., 1935–1938 (Tiny Betty) 275.00

    9" compo., 1936 only (Little Betty) 300.00

BELLE — 14", #18402, 1996 Dickens, red jacket, long skirt 125.00

BELLE BRUMMEL — Cloth, 1930s 775.00

BELLE OF THE BALL — 10", #1120, 1989 only, Portrette, deep rose gown (Cissette), 1997 . . . . 130.00

BELLE WATLING — 10", 1992 only, Scarlett Series (Cissette) 125.00

    21", #16277, 1995 only, red outfit with fur trim (Jacqueline) 350.00

BELLOWS' ANNE — 14" plastic/vinyl, #1568, 1987 only, Fine Arts Series 95.00

BELK & LEGGETT DEPARTMENT STORES — (see Special Events/Exclusives)

BERNHARDT, SARAH — 21", #2249, 1987 only, dressed in all burgundy. 325.00
BESSY BELL — 14" plastic/vinyl, #1565, 1988 only, Classic Series (Mary Ann) 75.00
BESSY BROOKS — 8", #487, 1988–1991, Storybook Series (Wendy Ann). 70.00
    8", 1990 (see Collectors United/Bride under Special Events/Exclusives). 100.00
BEST MAN — 8" h.p., #461, 1955 only (Wendy Ann) 750.00
BETH — (see Little Women)
    10" (see Spiegel's under Special Events/Exclusives) 125.00
BETTY — 14" compo., 1935–1942 . . . . 425.00
    12" compo., 1936–1937 only 350.00
    16–18" compo., 1935–1942 . . . . 425.00
    19–21" compo., 1938–1941 . . . . 550.00
    14½–17½" h.p., 1951 only, made for Sears (Maggie) 625.00
    30" plastic/vinyl, 1960 only 400.00
BETTY, TINY — 7" compo., 1934–1943 . . . . 350.00 up
BETTY, LITTLE — 9" compo., 1935–1943 . . . . 325.00 up
BETTY BAG — All cloth with flat painted face and yarn hair, 1940's 40.00
BETTY BLUE — 8" straight leg, #420, 1987–1988 only, Storybook Series (Maggie) 70.00
BIBLE CHARACTER DOLLS — 8" h.p., 1954 only, original box made like Bible (Wendy Ann) . . . . 6,500.00 up
    1995 (see Delilah, Joseph, Queen Esther, and Samson)
BILL/BILLY — 8" h.p., #320, #567, #420, 1955–1963, has boy's clothes and hair style (Wendy Ann) 550.00
    #577, 464, #466, #421, #442, #488, #388, 1953–1957, as groom . . . . 550.00 up
BILLIE HOLIDAY — 10", #22070, 1997, silver long gown 105.00
BILLY-IN-THE-BOX — 8" jester, 1996, Alexander signature box 95.00
BINNIE — 18" plastic/vinyl toddler, 1964 only 375.00
BINNIE WALKER — 15–18" h.p., 1954–1955 only (Cissy) 175.00–325.00
    15", 1955 only, in trunk with wardrobe 750.00
    15", 1955 only, h.p. skater . . . . 650.00 up
    18", toddler, plastic/vinyl, 1964 only . . . . 325.00 up
    25", 1955 only in formals, ... 500.00 up
    25", h.p., 1954–1955 only, dresses 450.00
BIRTHDAY DOLLS — 7" compo., 1937–1939 (Tiny Betty). . . . . 375.00 up

**12" BRENDA STARR, 1964, #920. Dressed for a Ball at
the Press Club. Mint in original box.**

BIRTHDAY, HAPPY — 1985 (see M.A.D.C. under Special Events/Exclusives) 325.00
BITSEY — 11–12" compo., 1942–1946. . . . . 275.00
    11–16" with h.p. head, 1949–1951. . . . . 185.00
    19–26", 1949–1951. . . . . 175.00–250.00
    12" cloth/vinyl, 1965–1966 only 150.00
BITSEY, LITTLE — 9" all vinyl, 1967–1968 only. 125.00
    11–16" 75.00–150.00
BLACK FOREST — 8", #512, 1989–1990 (Wendy Ann) 75.00
BLISS, BETTY TAYLOR — 1979–1981, 2nd set Presidents' Ladies/ First Ladies Series (Mary Ann) 125.00
BLUE BOY — 16" cloth, 1930's 650.00
    7" compo., 1936–1938 (Tiny Betty) 350.00
    9" compo., 1938–1941 (Little Betty) 400.00
    12" plastic/vinyl, #1340, 1972–1983, Portrait Children (Nancy Drew) 75.00
        1985–1987, dressed in blue velvet 85.00
    8", #22130, 1997, blue satin outfit 70.00
BLUE DANUBE — 18" h.p., 1953 only, pink floral gown (#2001B - blue floral gown) (Maggie) . . . . 1,600.00 up
    18" h.p., 1954 only, Me and My Shadow Series, blue taffeta dress (Margaret). . . . . 1,400.00 up
BLUE FAIRIE — 10", #1166, 1993 #201166, 1994, Portrette, character from Pinocchio (Cissette) 125.00
BLUE MOON — 14", #1560, 1991–1992 only, Classic Series (Louisa). 125.00
BLUE ZIRCON — 10", #1153, 1992 only, Birthday Collection, gold/blue flapper 85.00
BLYNKIN — (see Dutch Lullaby)
BOBBY — 8" h.p., #347, 1957 only (Wendy Ann) 600.00
    8" h.p., #361, #320, 1960 only (Maggie Mixup) 600.00
BOBBY Q. — Cloth, 1940–1942 . . . . 750.00
BOBBY (BOBBIE) SOXER — 8" h.p., 1990–1991 (see Disney under Special Events/Exclusives) 175.00
BOBO CLOWN — 8", #320, 1991–1992, Americana Series (Wendy Ann) 75.00
BOHEMIA — 8", #508, 1989–1991 (Wendy Ann) 60.00
BOLIVIA 8" h.p., BK & BKW, #786, 1963–1966 (Wendy Ann) 375.00
BONNET TOP WENDY — 8", #14487, 1995, Toy Shelf Series, yarn braids and large bonnet 65.00
BONNIE (BABY) — 16–19" vinyl, 1954–1955 . . . . 100.00
    24–30", 1954–1955. . . . . 150.00–250.00
BONNIE BLUE — 14", #1305, 1989 only, Jubilee II (Mary Ann) 125.00
    8" h.p., #629, #630, 1990–1992 (Wendy Ann) 95.00
    8", #16649, 1995, side saddle riding outfit 75.00
BONNIE GOES TO LONDON — 8", #640, 1993, Scarlett Series #160640-1994 . . . . 85.00
BONNIE TODDLER — 18" cloth/h.p. head/vinyl limbs, 1950–1951 . . . . 165.00
    19" all vinyl, 1954–1955 . . . . 200.00
    23–24" 250.00
BON VOYAGE — 8" and 10" (see I. Magnum under Special Events/Exclusives). 100.00–150.00
BOONE, DANIEL — 8" h.p., #315, 1991 only, Americana Series, has no knife (Wendy Ann) 65.00
BO PEEP, LITTLE — 7" compo., 1937–1941, Storybook Series (Tiny Betty) 375.00
    9–11" compo., 1936–1940 (Little Betty, Wendy Ann). 350.00
    7½" h.p., SLW, #489, 1955 only (Wendy Ann) 525.00
    8" h.p., BKW, #383, 1962–1964 (Wendy Ann) 250.00
    8" h.p., BK, #783, 1965–1972 (Wendy Ann). 125.00
    8" h.p., straight leg, #0783-483, 1973–1975, marked "Alex" (Wendy Ann) 75.00
    8" h.p., 1976–1986, #483–#486, marked "Alexander" (1985–1986 white face) (Wendy Ann) 65.00
    14", #1563, 1988–1989, Classic Series (Mary Ann) 75.00
    14", #1567, 1992–1993 only, candy stripe pink dress (Mary Ann). 135.00
    12" porcelain, #009, 1990–1992 . . . . 250.00
    10" Portrette series, 1994 . . . . 95.00
    8" (see Dolly Dears under Special Events/Exclusives) 250.00
BOYS CHOIR OF HARLEM — 8", #20170, 1997, maroon blazer, Kufi hat 75.00
BRAZIL — 7" compo., 1937–1943 (Tiny Betty) 325.00
    9" compo., 1938–1940 (Little Betty). 300.00

8" WENDY BRIDESMAID, 1955, #478. Straight leg walker.

BRAZIL, CONTINUED . . .

8" h.p., BKW, #773, 1965–1972 (Wendy Ann) 125.00
   BK, #773 . . . . 100.00
8" h.p., straight leg, #0773, #573, 1973–1975, marked "Alex." (Wendy Ann) 65.00
8" h.p., straight leg, #573, #547, #530, 1976–1988, marked "Alexander" 60.00
   #573, #547, #530, 1985–1987, white face 60.00
8" straight leg, #11564, 1996 international, carnival costume 75.00
BRENDA STARR — 12" h.p., 1964 only (became "Yolanda" in 1965) 250.00
   Bride. 325.00
   Street dresses 225.00
   Ball gown. 350.00
   Beach outfit 225.00
   Raincoat/hat/dress 250.00
BRIAR ROSE — (see M.A.D.C. under Special Events/Exclusives). 300.00
   10", #14101, 1995, Brothers Grimm Series, blue floral with apron (Cissette) 85.00
BRICK PIGGY — 12", #10010, 1997, denim overalls, maize felt cap. 85.00
BRIDE —
   TINY BETTY: Composition
      7" compo., 1935–1939 . . . . 275.00
      9–11" compo., 1936–1941 (Little Betty). 300.00
   WENDY ANN: Composition
      13", 14", 15" compo., 1935–1941 (Wendy Ann) 375.00
      17–18" compo., 1935–1943 (Wendy Ann) 450.00
      21–22" compo., 1942–1943 (Wendy Ann) . . . . 600.00 up
         In trunk/trousseau (Wendy Ann). . . . . 1,650.00 up
      21" compo., 1945–1947, Royal Wedding/Portrait (Wendy Ann). 2,400.00 up
   MARGARET, MAGGIE: Hard plastic
      15" h.p., 1951–1955 (Margaret) 650.00
      17" h.p., 1950, in pink (Margaret) 850.00
      18" h.p., tagged "Prin. Elizabeth" (Margaret) 675.00
      18" h.p., 1949–1955 (Maggie, Margaret). 650.00
      21" h.p., 1949–1953 (Margaret, Maggie). . . . . 1,200.00 up
      18"–21", pink bride, 1953 (Margaret) . . . . 900.00 up
      23" h.p. 1949, 1952–1955 (Margaret) 750.00
      25" h.p., 1955 only (Margaret) 800.00

BRIDE — MARY ANN, JENNIFER, LOUISA, *CONTINUED* . . .

    #1566, reintroduced 1992 only, ecru gown (Louisa, Jennifer) 150.00
   ELISE, LESLIE, POLLY: 17" plastic/vinyl or 21" porcelain
    1966–1988 (Elise) 150.00
    1966–1971 (Leslie). 275.00
    1965–1970 (Polly) 275.00
    Porcelain, 1989–1990, satin and lace look like bustle 475.00
    Porcelain, Portrait Series, 1993–1994 . . . . 475.00
BRIDESMAID — 9" compo., 1937–1939 (Little Betty) 325.00
   11–14" compo., 1938–1942 (Wendy Ann) 350.00–450.00
   15–18" compo., 1939–1944 (Wendy Ann) 375.00–575.00
   20–22" compo., 1941–1947, Portrait (Wendy Ann) . . . . 1,800.00 up
   21½" compo., 1938–1941 (Princess Elizabeth). 950.00
   15–17" h.p., 1950–1952 (Margaret, Maggie) 450.00–600.00
   15" h.p., 1952 (Maggie) 525.00
   18" h.p., 1952 (Maggie) 650.00
   21" h.p., 1950–1953, side part mohair wig, deep pink or lavender gown (Margaret) . . . . 700.00 up
   19" rigid vinyl, in pink, 1952–1953 (Margaret) 550.00
   15" h.p., 1955 only (Cissy, Binnie) 325.00
   18" h.p., 1955 only (Cissy, Binnie) 350.00
   25" h.p., 1955 only (Cissy, Binnie) 450.00
   20" h.p., 1956 only, Fashion Parade Series, blue nylon tulle & net (Cissy) 1,000.00
   10" h.p., 1957–1963 (Cissette) 375.00
   12" h.p., 1956–1959 (Lissy). . . . . 600.00 up
   16½" h.p., 1957–1959 (Elise) . . . . 450.00 up
   8" h.p., SLW, #478, 1955 (Wendy Ann) . . . . 700.00 up
     BKW, #621, 1956 . . . . 675.00 up
     BKW, #408, #583, #445, 1957–1959 . . . . 700.00 up
   17" plastic/vinyl, (Elise) 1966–1987. . . . . 175.00
   17" plastic/vinyl, 1966–1971 (Leslie). 275.00
BRIGITTA — 11" & 14" (see Sound of Music)
BROOKE — (see FAO Schwarz under Special Events/Exclusives) 125.00
BUBBLES CLOWN — 8" h.p., #342, 1993–1994, Americana Series 75.00
BUCK RABBIT — Cloth/felt, 1930's . . . . 650.00 up
BUD — 16–19" cloth/vinyl, 1952 only (Rosebud head). 150.00
   19" & 25", 1952–1953 only. 175.00–275.00
BULGARIA — 8", #557, 1986–1987, white face (Wendy Ann) 60.00
BUMBLE BEE — 8" h.p., #323, 1992–1993, only Americana Series 65.00
BUNNY — 18" plastic/vinyl, 1962 only, mint 250.00
BURMA — 7" compo., 1939–1943 (Tiny Betty) 350.00
BUTCH — 11–12" compo./cloth, 1942–1946 . . . . 150.00
   14–16" compo./cloth, 1949–1951 . . . . 175.00
   14" cloth, vinyl head & limbs, 1950 only 175.00
   12" cloth/vinyl, 1965–1966 only 95.00
BUTCH, LITTLE — 9" all vinyl, 1967–1968 only 125.00
BUTCH McGUFFEY — 22" compo./cloth, 1940–1941 . . . . 275.00

Please read "What is a Price Guide?" for additional information.

C.U. — (see Collectors United under Special Events/Exclusives)
CAFE ROSE AND IVORY COCKTAIL DRESS — 10", #22200 – white, #22203 – black, 1997. . . . . 115.00
CALAMITY JANE — 8" h.p. Americana Series, 1994 only (Wendy Ann) 65.00
CAMEO LADY — (see Collectors United under Special Events/Exclusives) 125.00
CAMELOT — (see Collectors United under Special Events/Exclusives) 125.00
CAMILLE — 21" compo., 1938–1939 (Wendy Ann) 3,500.00
CANADA — 8" h.p., BK, #760, 1968–1972 (Wendy Ann) 100.00
   Straight leg, #0706, 1973–1975, marked "Alex." 65.00
   Straight legs, #560 (#534 in 1986), 1976–1988, (white face 1985–1987), marked "Alexander" 60.00
CANDY KID — 11–15" compo., 1938–1941 (Wendy Ann) red/white stripe dress 275.00–450.00
CAPTAIN HOOK — 8" h.p., #478, 1992–1993 only, Storyland Series (Peter Pan) (Wendy Ann) 80.00
CAREEN — (see Carreen)
CARMEN — Dressed like Carmen Miranda, but not marked or meant as such.
   7" compo., 1938–1943 (Tiny Betty) 350.00
   9–11" compo., 1938–1943, boy & girl (see also "Rumbera/Rumbero") (Little Betty) . . . . 275.00 each
   11" compo., 1937–1939, has sleep eyes (Little Betty). 350.00
   14" compo., 1937–1940 (Wendy Ann) 425.00
   17" compo., 1939–1942 (Wendy Ann) 650.00
   21" compo., 1939–1942, extra makeup, mint (Wendy Ann) 1,400.00
   21" compo., 1939–1942, Portrait with extra make-up . . . . 1,850.00 up
   14" plastic/vinyl, #1410, 1983–1986, Opera Series (Mary Ann). 80.00
   10" h.p., #1154, 1993 only, Portrette Series (Miranda), yellow/red 90.00
CARNAVALE DOLL — (see FAO Schwarz under Special Events/Exclusives) 185.00
CARNIVAL IN RIO — 21" porcelain, 1989–1990 . . . . 500.00
CARNIVAL IN VENICE — 21" porcelain, 1990–1991 . . . . 500.00
CAROLINE — 15" vinyl, 1961–1962 only, in dresses, pants/jacket. 350.00
   In riding habit 375.00
   Dressed as Kurt of Sound of Music 475.00
   In case/wardrobe. . . . . 900.00 up
   8", 1993 (see Belk & Leggett under Special Events/Exclusives) 100.00
   8", 1994 (see Neiman-Marcus under Special Events/Exclusives) 250.00
CARREEN/CAREEN — 14–17" compo., #1593, 1937–1938 (Wendy Ann) . . . . 700.00 up
   14" plastic/vinyl, 1992–1993 only (Louisa/Jennifer) 125.00

10" CISSETTE, 1957, #909. A summer cotton dress and straw hat with flowers.

16½" COUNTRY COUSIN, 1958. "Marybel" face. Plastic/vinyl.

Carmen, continued . . .

8" plaid, two large ruffles at hem, #160646, 1994 only 75.00
CARROT KATE — 14", #25506, 1995, Ribbons & Bows Series, vegetable print dress (Mary Ann) 150.00
CARROT TOP — 21" cloth, 1967 only 125.00
CASEY JONES — 8" h.p., 1991–1992 only, Americana Series 65.00
CATERPILLAR — 8" h.p., #14594, 1995 – 1996, has eight legs, Alice In Wonderland Series 75.00
CATS — 16", plush, dressed, glass eyes, long lashes, felt nose 350.00
CAT ON A HOT TIN ROOF — 10", #20011, "Maggie," white chiffon dress 115.00
CELIA'S DOLLS — (see Special Events/Exclusives)
CENTURY OF FASHION — 14" & 18" h.p., 1954 (Margaret, Maggie & Cissy) . . . . 1,800.00 up
CHANGING SEASONS — (Spring, Summer, Autumn, Winter) 14" 1993–1994 . . . . 150.00 each
CHARITY — 8" h.p., #485, 1961 only, Americana Series, blue cotton dress (Wendy Ann) . . . . 1,800.00 up
CHAMPS-ELYSÉES — 21" h.p., black lace over pink, rhinestone on cheek. . . . . 4,800.00 up
CHARLENE — 18" cloth/vinyl, 1991–1992 only 100.00
CHATTERBOX — 24" plastic/vinyl talker, 1961 only . . . . 275.00 up
CHEERLEADER — 8", #324, 1990–1991 only, Americana Series (Wendy Ann) 65.00
8", 1990 (see I. Magnin under Special Events/Exclusives). 85.00
8" h.p., #324, #324-1, 1992–1993 only, Americana Series, black or white doll, royal blue/gold outfit . . . 60.00
CHERI — 18" h.p., 1954 only, Me and My Shadow Series, white satin gown, pink opera coat (Margaret). . 1,600.00
CHERRY BLOSSOM — 14", #25504, 1995, Ribbons & Bows Series, cherry print dress (Mary Ann) 135.00
CHERRY TWINS — 8" h.p., #388E, 1957 only (Wendy Ann) . . . . 1,500.00 up each
CHERUB — 12" vinyl, 1960–1961 . . . . 250.00
18" h.p. head/cloth & vinyl, 1950's 350.00
26", 1950's 375.00
CHERUB BABIES — Cloth, 1930's 450.00
CHESHIRE CAT — 8", #13070, 1997, pink velvet cat suit 60.00
CHILE — 8" h.p., #528, 1992 only (Wendy Ann). 65.00
CHILD AT HEART SHOP — (see Special Events/Exclusives)
CHILD'S ANGEL — 8", #14701, 1996, gold wings, harp, halo 65.00
CHINA — 7" compo., 1936–1940 (Tiny Betty) 300.00
9" compo., 1935–1938 (Little Betty) 275.00
8" h.p., BK, #772, 1972 (Wendy Ann) 100.00
8" (Maggie smile face) 125.00
Straight leg, #0772–#572, 1973–1975, marked "Alex." 70.00
Straight leg, #572, 1976–1986, marked "Alexander" (Wendy Ann) 65.00
#572, 1987–1989 (Maggie) 65.00
8", #11550, 1995 only, 3 painted lashes at edge of eyes (Wendy Ann) 60.00
8", #11561, 1996 International, Little Empress costume 75.00
CHINESE NEW YEAR — 8", 2 dolls, #21040, 1997 . . . . 130.00
8", 3 dolls, dragon, #21050, 1997. . . . . 230.00
CHRISTENING BABY — 11–13" cloth/vinyl, 1951–1954. . . . . 125.00
16–19" 150.00
CHRISTMAS ANGELS — (see Tree Toppers)
CHRISTMAS CANDY — 14" #1544, 1993 only, Classic Series. 115.00
CHRISTMAS CAROL — 8" (see Saks Fifth Avenue under Special Events/Exclusives) 100.00
CHRISTMAS CAROLER — 8" #19650, 1997, red velvet cape, print skirt 85.00
CHRISTMAS CAROLING — 10", #1149, 1992–1993 only, Portrette, burnt orange/gold dress 115.00
CHRISTMAS COOKIE — 14", #1565, 1992 (Also see Lil Christmas Cookie, 8") (Louisa/Jennifer) 125.00
CHRISTMAS EVE — 14" plastic/vinyl #241594, 1994 only (Mary Ann). 115.00
8", #10364, 1995, Christmas Series 70.00
CHRISTMAS SHOPPE — (see Special Events/Exclusives)
CHRISTMAS TREE TOPPER — 8" (see Spiegel's under Special Events/Exclusives; also Tree Topper) 150.00
CHURCHILL, LADY — 18" h.p., #2020C, 1953 only, Beaux Arts Series,
pink gown with full opera coat (Margaret). . . . . 2,200.00 up
CHURCHILL, SIR WINSTON — 18" h.p., 1953 only, has hat (Margaret) 1,200.00

CINDERELLA — (see also Topsy Turvy for two headed version)

7–8" compo., 1935–1944 (Tiny Betty) 295.00
9" compo., 1936–1941 (Little Betty) 350.00
13" compo., 1935–1937 (Wendy Ann) 375.00
14" compo., 1939 only, Sears exclusive (Princess Elizabeth) 500.00
15" compo., 1935–1937 (Betty) 475.00
16–18" compo., 1935–1939 (Princess Elizabeth) . . . . 500.00 up
8" h.p., #402, 1955 only (Wendy Ann) 950.00
8" h.p., #498, 1990–1991, Storyland Series (Wendy Ann) 65.00
8", #476, 1992–1993, blue ballgown, #140476, 1994 Storyland Series 75.00
8", #475, 1992 only, "Poor" outfit in blue w/black strips 70.00
8" h.p., #14540, 1995 – 1996, pink net gown with roses, Brothers Grimm Series 1995-1996, #13400, 1997 . . 65.00
8", h.p., #13410, 1997, calico skirt with broom and pumpkin 75.00
12" h.p., 1966 only, Literature Series (classic Lissy) 900.00
12" h.p., 1966, "Poor" outfit 650.00
     1966, in window box with both outfits 1,500.00
14" h.p., 1950–1951, ballgown (Margaret) . . . . 850.00 up
14" h.p., 1950–1951, "Poor" outfit (Margaret) 600.00
18" h.p., 1950–1951 (Margaret) 750.00
21", #45501, 1995, pink and blue, Madame's Portfolio Series 325.00
14" plastic/vinyl, (#1440 to 1974; #1504 to 1991; #1541 in 1992) 1967–1992, "Poor" outfit
     (can be green, blue, gray or brown) (Mary Ann) 80.00
14", #140 on box, 1969 only, FAO Schwarz, all blue satin/gold trim, mint (Mary Ann) 425.00
14" plastic/vinyl, #1445, #1446, #1546, #1548, 1970–1983, Classic Series, dressed in pink (Mary Ann) 125.00
     #1548, #1549, 1984–1986, blue ballgown, two styles (Mary Ann) 125.00
14", #1546, #1547, 1987–1991, Classic Series, white or blue ballgown (Mary Ann, Jennifer) 150.00
14", #1549, 1992 only, white/gold ballgown (Jennifer) 150.00
14", 1985, with trunk (see Enchanted Dollhouse under Special Events/Exclusives) 275.00

10" CISSETTE, 1957, #976. All hard plastic. Short theatre dress and coat. Came in different colors. Hard to find in pink.

10" CISSETTE, 1961, #806. Hard plastic. Cotton one-piece sunsuit with removable skirt. Has a basket instead of hatbox.

CINDERELLA, CONTINUED . . .

    14", 1994, has two outfits (see Disney World under Special Events/Exclusives) 200.00
    14", 1996, #87002, white gown, gold crown (Mary Ann) 125.00
    10", 1989 (see Disney Annual Showcase of Dolls under Special Events/Exclusives) 700.00
    10", #1137, 1990–1991, Portrette, dressed in all pink (Cissette) 95.00

CISSETTE — 10–11" h.p., 1957–1963, high heel feet, jointed elbows & knees, must have good face color,
in various street dresses. Allow more for M.I.B., rare outfits & fancy hairdos. 275.00
    In formals, ballgowns . . . . 475.00 up
    Coats & hats 325.00
    1961 only, beauty queen with trophy 350.00
    Special gift set/three wigs 900.00
        Doll only, clean with good face color 125.00
    1954, Queen/trunk/trousseau 1,200.00
        Slacks or pants outfits 250.00

CISSY — 20" h.p. (also 21"), 1955–1959, jointed elbows & knees, high heel feet, must have good
face color, in various street dresses 375.00
    Dress & full length coat 425.00
    In ballgowns . . . . 850.00 up
    Trunk/wardrobe . . . . 1,300.00 up
    Pants suits 275.00
    1950s magazine ads using doll (add 10.00 if framed) 20.00
    21", reintroduced in the following 1996 MA Couture Collection
        #67303, aquamarine evening column and coat 275.00

DATING CISSETTE DOLLS

EYELIDS: 1975 - beige; 1958 - pale pink; 1959–1963 - peach

CLOTHES: 1957–1958 - darts in bodice; 1959–1963 - no darts except ballgowns

FINGERNAILS: 1962–1963 - polished

EYEBROWS: 1957–1963 - single stroked

BODY AND LEGS: 1957–1963 - head strung with hook and rubber band; legs jointed with plastic socket

FEET: 1957–1963 - high heels

WIGS: 1957–1958 - three rows of stitching; 1959–1963 - zigzag stitches except 1961–1962 with fancy hairdos, then three rows; 1963 - few have rooted hair in cap, glued to head or removable wigs

TAGS: 1957–1962 - turquoise; 1963 - dark blue

PORTRETTE: 1968–1973
Two or three stroke eyebrows, blue eyelids, no earrings, strung head with hook, high heels.

JACQUELINE: 1961–1962
Two or three stroke eyebrows, side seam brunette wig, small curl on forehead, blue eyelids, eyeliner, painted lashes to sides of eyes, polished nails, head strung, socket jointed hips with side seams, high heels.

SLEEPING BEAUTY: 1959 ONLY
3 stroke eyebrows, pink eyelids, no earrings, mouth painted wider, no knee joints, flat feet, jointed with metal hooks.

SOUND OF MUSIC: 1971–1973
(Brigetta, Liesl, Louisa)
Two stroke eyebrows, the rest same as Portrettes.

TINKERBELLE: 1969 ONLY
Two stroke eyebrows, blue eyelids, painted lashes to side of eyes, no earrings, hair rooted into wig cap, head and legs strung with metal hooks.

MARGOT: 1961
Same as Jacqueline, except has three stroke eyebrows and elaborate hairdos.

CISSY, CONTINUED . . .

#67307, aquamarine evening column and coat, African-American 275.00
#67302, cafe rose and ivory cocktail dress 325.00
#67306, cafe rose and ivory cocktail dress, African-American 325.00
#67301, coral and leopard travel ensemble 325.00
#67305, coral and leopard travel ensemble, African-American 325.00
#67601, ebony and ivory houndstooth suit 350.00
#67603, ebony and ivory houndstooth suit, African-American 350.00
#67304, onyx velvet lace gala gown and coat 350.00
#67308, onyx velvet lace gala gown and coat, African-American 350.00
#67602, pearl embroidered lace bridal gown. 625.00
#67604, pearl embroidered lace bridal gown, African-American 625.00
#86003, limited edition red sequined gown 350.00
21", 1997 MA Coutre Collection
#22210, daisy resort ensemble. 375.00
#22230, tea rose cocktail ensemble 325.00
#22220, calla lily evening ensemble 690.00
#22240, peony and butterfly wedding gown 425.00
#22290, gardenia gala ball gown 375.00
#22250, Cissy's secret armoire trunk set 735.00
CISSY BRIDE — 21", #52011, porcelain portrait, 1994 only 500.00
CISSY BY SCASSI — (see FAO Schwarz under Special Events/Exclusives) 375.00
CISSY GODEY BRIDE 21", #011, porcelain, 1993 only 525.00
CIVIL WAR — 18" h.p., #2010B, 1953 only, Glamour Girls Series, white taffeta with red roses (Margaret) . . 1,400.00
CLARA & THE NUTCRACKER — 14", #1564, 1992 only (Louisa/Jennifer) 110.00

18" SIR WINSTON CHURCHILL, 1953. Hard plastic.

21" CISSY EBONY AND IVORY, 1996. MA Couture Collection, #67601.

CLARA'S PARTY DRESS — 8", #14570, 1995, Nutcracker Series...............................65.00
CLARABELL CLOWN — 19", 1951–1953..350.00
    29"...575.00
    49"...1,000.00
CLAUDETTE — 10", #1123 (in peach), 1988–1989, Portrette (Cissette) 95.00
CLEOPATRA — 12", #1315, 1980–1985, Portraits of History Series 75.00
    10", #86002, 1996 Platinum Collection 105.00
CLEVELAND, FRANCES — 1985–1987, 4th set Presidents' Ladies/First Ladies Series (Mary Ann)..........125.00
CLOVER KID — 7" compo., 1935–1936 (Tiny Betty) 375.00
CLOWN — 8", #305, 1990–1992 only, Americana Series, has painted face (Maggie) 75.00
    BABY — 8", #464-1955, has painted face (Wendy Ann) ....1,200.00 up
    BOBO — 8" h.p., #310, 1991–1992 (Wendy Ann) 85.00
    PIERROT — 8", #561, 1956 only (Wendy Ann) ....1,000.00 up
      14", 1991 only, #1558, white costume with red trim...................85.00
    STILTS — 8" #320, 1992–1993, doll on stilts............................70.00
COCA COLA CARHOP — 10", #17400, 1997, roller skates 115.00
COCA COLA FANTASY — 10", #31210 – white, #31213 – black, 1997 ....155.00
COCO — 21" plastic/vinyl, 1966, in various clothes (other than Portrait)..........2,000.00 up
    In sheath style ballgown ....2,200.00 up
    14", #1558, 1991–1992, Classic Series (Mary Ann) 85.00
    10", #1140, 1989–1992, Portrette, dressed in all black (Cissette) 75.00
    16", #31240, 1997, travel wardrobe and dog, Cleo.....................425.00
COLLECTORS UNITED — (see Special Events/Exclusives)
COLLEEN — 10", #1121, 1988 only, Portrette, in green (Cissette) 80.00
COLONIAL — 7" compo., 1937–1938 (Tiny Betty) 300.00
    9" compo., 1936–1939 (Little Betty).................................300.00
    8" h.p., BKW, #389, #789, 1962–1964 (Wendy Ann) 325.00

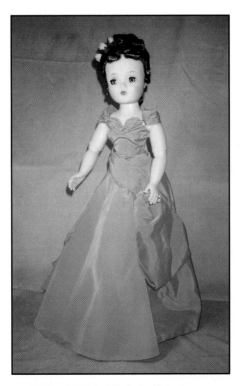

21" CISSY, 1956, #2036. Pink taffeta torso gown with side drapery held in place by jeweled ornaments. Replaced flowers in hair.

COLUMBIAN SAILOR — (see U.F.D.C. under Special Events/Exclusives)..................250.00
COLUMBINE — 8", #14575-1995, Nutcracker Series..................65.00
COLUMBUS, CHRISTOPHER — 8" h.p., #328, 1992 only, Americana Series..................125.00
COMEDIENNE — 10", #20120, clown, 1996 Cirque du Soleil Series..................85.00
CONFEDERATE OFFICER — 12", 1990–1991, Scarlett Series (Wendy Ann)..................80.00
    8" h.p., 1991–1992, Scarlett Series (see Ashley)
COOKIE — 19" compo./cloth, 1938–1940, must be in excellent condition..................650.00
COOLIDGE, GRACE — 14", 1989–1990, 6th set Presidents' Ladies/First Ladies Series (Louisa)..................125.00
CORAL AND LEOPARD TRAVEL ENSEMBLE — 10", #22180, 1997..................115.00
CORNELIA — Cloth & felt, 1930s..................700.00 up
    21", #2191, 1972, Portrait, dressed in pink with full cape (Jacqueline)..................450.00
    #2191, 1973, pink with ¾ length jacket..................375.00
    #2296, 1974, blue with black trim..................350.00
    #2290, 1975, rose red with black trim and hat..................350.00
    #2293, 1976, pink with black trim and hat..................325.00
    #2212, 1978, blue with full cape..................325.00
COSSACK — 8" h.p. #511, 1989–1991 (Wendy Ann)..................70.00
COUNTRY CHRISTMAS — 14", #1543, 1991–1992 only, Classic Series (Mary Ann)..................150.00
COUNTRY COUSINS — 10" cloth, 1940s..................575.00
    26" cloth, 1940s..................650.00
    30" cloth, 1940s..................750.00
    16½", 1958, mint (Marybel)..................375.00
COUNTRY FAIR — (see Wendy Loves)
COURTNEY AND FRIENDS — (see Madame Alexander Doll Company under Special Events/Exclusives)...725.00 set
COUSIN GRACE — 8" h.p., BKW, #432, 1957 only (Wendy Ann)..................1,800.00 up
COUSIN KAREN — 8" h.p., BKW, #620, 1956 only (Wendy Ann)..................1,600.00 up
COUSIN MARIE & MARY — 8" h.p. (Marie - #465; Mary - #462) 1963 only (Wendy Ann)..................1,000.00 each
COWARDLY LION — 8", #431, 1993, Storybook Series #140431-1994–1996, #13220-1997..................60.00
COWBOY — 8" h.p., BK, #732, 1967–1969, Americana Series (Wendy Ann)..................425.00
    8", 1987 (see M.A.D.C. under Special Events/Exclusives)..................425.00
COWGIRL — 8" h.p., BK, #724, 1967–1970, Americana/Storybook Series (Wendy Ann)..................425.00
    10", #1132, 1990–1991, Portrette, white/red outfit (Cissette)..................75.00
CRETE — 8" straight leg, #529, 1987 only (white face)..................70.00
CROATIA — 8", h.p., #110543, 1994 (Wendy Ann)..................70.00
CROCKETT, DAVY, BOY OR GIRL — 8" h.p., 1955 only (Boy - #446; Girl - #443) (Wendy Ann)..................700.00 up
CRY DOLLY — 14–16" vinyl, 1953, 12-piece layette..................225.00
    14", 16", 19" in swimsuit..................100.00–175.00
    16–19" all vinyl, dress or rompers..................150.00–175.00
CUBA — 8", #11548, 1995 only, has round brown face..................60.00
CUDDLY — 10½" cloth, 1942–1944..................375.00
    17" cloth, 1942–1944..................400.00
CURLY LOCKS — 8" h.p., #472, 1955 only (Wendy Ann)..................850.00 up
    8" straight leg, #421, 1987–1988, Storybook Series, 1997..................85.00
CUTE LITTLE BABY — 14", 1994–1995, doll only..................100.00   With layette and basket...225.00
CYNTHIA — 15" h.p., 1952 only (black "Margaret")..................850.00 up
    18", 1952 only..................950.00 up
    23", 1952 only..................1,200.00
CYRANO — 8" h.p., #140505, 1994 only, Storyland Series (Pinocchio)..................70.00
CZECHOSLOVAKIA — 7" compo., 1935–1937 (Tiny Betty)..................300.00
    8" h.p., BK, #764, 1972 (Wendy Ann)..................125.00
    Straight leg, #0764, #564, 1973–1975, marked "Alex"..................65.00
    Straight leg, #536, 1976–1987, marked "Alexander"..................55.00
    8", #536, 1985–1987, white face..................55.00
    8", #521, reintroduced 1992–1993 only (Wendy Ann)..................55.00

Please read "What is a Price Guide?" for additional information.

DAFFY DOWN DILLY — 8" straight legs, #429, 1986 only, Storybook Series (Wendy Ann) 75.00
DAHL, ARLENE (PINK CHAMPAGNE) — 18" h.p., 1950–1951, red wig, lavender gown (Maggie)   mint . . . .5,500.00 up
DAISY — 10", #1110, 1987–1989, Portrette series, white lace over yellow (Cissette) 75.00
DANISH — 7" compo., 1937–1941 (Tiny Betty) 325.00
    9" compo., 1938–1940 (Little Betty) 350.00
DARE, VIRGINIA — 9" compo., 1940–1941 (Little Betty) 450.00
DARLENE — 18" cloth/vinyl, 1991–1992 . . . . .100.00
DAVID AND DIANE — 8", (see FAO Schwarz under Special Events/Exclusives) .175.00
DAVID COPPERFIELD — 7" compo., 1936–1938 (Tiny Betty) 350.00
    14" compo., 1938 only (Wendy Ann) 700.00
    16" cloth, early 1930s, Dicken's character . . . . .800.00 up
DAVID, THE LITTLE RABBI — 8", (see Celia's Dolls under Special Events/Exclusives) 75.00
DAVID QUACK-A-FIELD OR TWISTAIL — Cloth/felt, 1930's . . . . .700.00 up
DAY OF WEEK DOLLS — 7", 1935–1940 (Tiny Betty) . . . . .350.00 each
    9–11" compo., 1936–1938 (Little Betty) . . . . .375.00 each
    13" compo., 1939 (Wendy Ann) 425.00
DEAREST — 12" vinyl baby, 1962–1964 . . . . .150.00
DEBRA (DEBORAH) — 21", 1949–1951, Portrette, ballerina with extra make-up (Margaret) . . . . .5,000.00 up
    21", 1949–1951, bride with five-piece layered bustle in back . . . . .5,000.00 up
DEBUTANTE — 18" h.p., 1953 only (Maggie) . . . . .1,250.00 up
DECEMBER — 14", #1528, 1989 only, Classic Series (Mary Ann) .95.00
DEFOE, DR. ALLEN — 14–15" compo., 1937–1939 . . . . .1,600.00 up
DEGAS — 21" compo., 1945–1946, Portrait (Wendy Ann) . . . . .2,250.00 up
DEGAS "DANCE LESSON" — 14" #241598, 1994 . . . . .95.00

21" DEBRA BRIDE, 1950. "Margaret" face. All hard plastic. A very unusual gown with a five-piece layered bustle. An extremely rare doll.

DEGAS GIRL — 14", #1475 (#1575 from 1974), 1967–1987 (20 year production), Portrait Children and
Fine Arts Series (Mary Ann) 75.00
DELILAH — 8" h.p., #14583, 1995 only, Bible Series 85.00
DENMARK — 10" h.p., 1962–1963 (Cissette) 650.00
    8" h.p., BK, #769, 1970–1972 (Wendy Ann) 100.00
    8" h.p., straight leg, #0769-569, 1973–1975, marked "Alex." (Wendy Ann) 75.00
    8" h.p., straight leg, #546, 1976–1989, marked "Alexander" (1985–1987 white face) (Wendy Ann) 65.00
    8" reintroduced, #519, 1991 only (Wendy Ann) 55.00
DESERT STORM — (see Welcome Home)
DIANA — 14", 1993–1994, Anne of Green Gables Series, trunk and wardrobe 275.00
    Tea dress, came with tea set 1993 only 150.00
    Sunday Social 8" #260417, 1994-1995 (Wendy Ann) 70.00
    Sunday Social 14" #261503, 1994 . . . . .125.00
DIAMOND LIL — 10" (see M.A.D.C. under Special Events/Exclusives) .300.00
DICKINSON, EMILY — 14", #1587, 1989 only, Classic Series (Mary Ann) 95.00
DICKSIE & DUCKSIE — Cloth/felt, 1930's . . . . .700.00 up
DILLY DALLY SALLY — 7" compo., 1937–1942 (Tiny Betty) 300.00
    9" compo., 1938–1939 (Little Betty) 325.00
DING DONG BELL — 7" compo., 1937–1942 (Tiny Betty) 325.00
DINNER AT EIGHT — 10", #1127, 1989–1991, Portrette, black/white dress (Cissette) 75.00
DINOSAUR — 8" h.p., #343, 1993–1994, Americana Series 65.00
DIONNE QUINTS — Original mint or very slight craze.
    Each has own color: Yvonne–pink, Annette–yellow, Cecile–green, Emilie–lavender, Marie–blue
    20" compo. toddlers, 1938–1939 . . . . .700.00 each   4,200.00 set
    19" compo. toddlers, 1936–1938 . . . . .700.00 each   4,200.00 set
    16–17" compo. toddlers, 1937–1939 . . . . .650.00 each   3,600.00 set
    14" compo. toddlers, 1937–1938 . . . . .500.00 each   2,500.00 set
    11" compo. toddlers, 1937–1938, wigs & sleep eyes . . . . .400.00 each   2,200.00 set
    11" compo. toddlers, 1937–1938, molded hair & sleep eyes . . . . .400.00 each   2,200.00 set
    11" compo. babies, 1936, wigs & sleep eyes . . . . .400.00 each   2,200.00 set
    11" compo. babies, 1936, molded hair & sleep eyes . . . . .400.00 each   2,200.00 set
    8" compo. toddlers, 1935–1939, molded hair or wigs & painted eyes . . . . .250.00 each   1,200.00 set
    8" compo. babies, 1935–1939, molded hair or wigs & painted eyes . . . . .300.00 each   1,400.00 set

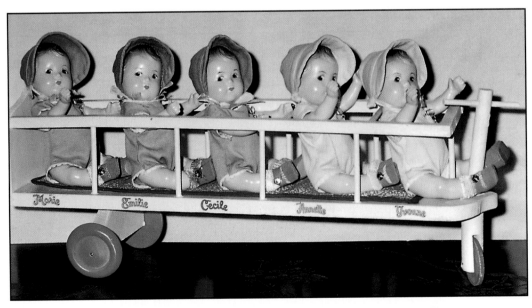

8" DIONNE QUINTS, 1935–39. All composition. Original stroller.

DIONNE QUINTS, CONTINUED . . .

14" cloth/compo., 1938	.475.00 each	3,100.00 set
17" cloth/compo., 1938	.575.00 each	3,600.00 set
22" cloth/compo., 1936–1937		.700.00 each
24" all cloth, 1935–1936, must be mint		1,200.00 each
16" all cloth, 1935–1936, must be mint		900.00 up

DIONNE FURNITURE — (NO DOLLS)

Scooter, holds 5	.300.00 up
Basket case, holds 5	.200.00
Divided high chair, holds 5	.250.00 up
Table and chairs, 5 piece set	.400.00
Ferris wheel, holds 5	.350.00 up
Bath/shower	.250.00 up
Wagon, holds 5	.400.00 up
Playpen, holds 5	.250.00 up
Crib, holds 5	.250.00 up
Tricycle	125.00 each
Merry-go-round, holds 5	.350.00 up
High chair for 1	.100.00

DISNEY — (see Special Events/Exclusives)

DOGS — (see Poodles)

DOLL FINDERS — (see Special Events/Exclusives)

DOLLS OF THE MONTH — 7–8" compo., 1937–1939, Birthday Dolls (Tiny Betty) 325.00

DOLLS 'N BEARLAND — (see Special Events/Exclusives)

DOLLY — 8", #436, 1988–1989, Storybook Series (Wendy Ann), 1997 . . . . .85.00

DOLLY DEARS — (see Special Events/Exclusives)

DOLLY DRYPER — 11" vinyl, 1952 only, 7-piece layette 325.00

DOLLY LEVI (MATCHMAKER) — 10" Portrette, 1994 only 75.00

DOMINICAN REPUBLIC — 8" straight leg, #544, 1986–1988 (1985–1986 white face) 65.00

DOROTHY — 14", #1532, 1990–1993, all blue/white check dress and solid blue pinafore (Mary Ann) 85.00

    8" h.p., #464, 1991–1993, #140464, 1994–1995, blue/white check, white bodice (Wendy Ann) 55.00

    8" h.p., emerald green dress special, mid-year special

        (see Madame Alexander Doll Co. under Special Events/Exclusives) 65.00

    8" h.p., #13200, 1997, blue check dress 60.00

    14" plastic/vinyl, #87007, 1996 . . . . .125.00

DOTTIE DUMBUNNIE — Cloth/felt, 1930s . . . . .800.00 up

DRESSED FOR OPERA — 18" h.p., 1953 only (Margaret) . . . . .1,800.00 up

DRESSED LIKE DADDY — 8", #17002, 1996, white or black 65.00

DRESSED LIKE MOMMY — 8", #17001, 1996, white or black 60.00

DRUCILLA — (see M.A.D.C. under Special Events/Exclusives) 175.00

DRUM MAJORETTE — (see Majorette)

DUCHESS, THE — 8", #14613, 1996, Alice in Wonderland series 72.00

DUCHESS ELIZA, THE — 10", #20114, 1996 classics 115.00

DUDE RANCH — 8" h.p., #449, 1955 only (Wendy Ann) . . . . .700.00 up

DUMPLIN' BABY — 20–23½", 1957–1958 . . . . .185.00

DUTCH — 7" compo., 1935–1939 (Tiny Betty) 300.00

    9" compo boy or girl, 1936–1941 . . . . .325.00

    8" h.p., BKW, #777, 1964, boy* (Wendy Ann) 125.00

        BK, #777, #0777, 1965–1972 . . . . .100.00

        8" h.p., straight leg, #777, *0777, 1972–1973, marked "Alex" 75.00

    8" h.p., BKW, #391-791, 1961–1964, girl* 125.00

        8" h.p. BK, #791, 1965–1972 . . . . .100.00

        8" BKW, #791, 1964 only (Maggie smile face) 125.00

DUTCH LULLABY — 8", #499, 1993, #140499, 1994, Wynkin, Blynkin & Nod, in wooden shoe. 200.00

* BOTH BECAME NETHERLANDS IN 1974.

Please read "What is a Price Guide?" for additional information.

EASTER BONNET — 14", #1562, 1992 (Louisa/Jennifer) 150.00
    8" h.p., #10383–10385, 1995-1996, three hair colors, Special Occasions Series 62.00
    8", h.p., #10401, 1996, African-American 62.00
EASTER BUNNY 8" (see Child at Heart under Special Events/Exclusives) 350.00
EASTER DOLL 8" h.p., 1968 only, special for West Coast, in yellow dress (Wendy Ann) . . . . .1,100.00 up
    7½", SLNW, #361, 1953, organdy dress, doll carries basket with chicken . . . . .925.00 up
    14" plastic/vinyl, 1968 only (Mary Ann) . . . . .600.00 up
EASTER OF YESTERDAY — 1995 (see C.U. under Special Events/Exclusives) .75.00
EASTER SUNDAY — 8" h.p., #340 or #340-1, 1993 only, Americana Series, black or white doll 70.00
EBONY AND IVORY HOUNDSTOOTH SUIT — 10", #22190, 1997 . . . . .115.00
ECUADOR — 8" h.p., BK & BKW, #878, 1963–1966 (Wendy Ann) 350.00
EDITH, THE LONELY DOLL — 16" plastic/vinyl, 1958–1959 . . . . .375.00
    22", 1958–1959 . . . . .400.00
    8" h.p., #850, 1958 only (Wendy Ann) . . . . .750.00 up
EDITH WITH GOLDEN HAIR — 18" cloth, 1940's 675.00
EDWARDIAN — 18" h.p., #2001A, 1953 only, pink embossed cotton, Glamour Girl Series (Margaret) 1,500.00
    8" h.p., #0200, 1953 only (Wendy Ann) 950.00
EISENHOWER, MAMIE — 14", 1989–1990, 6th set Presidents' Ladies/First Ladies Series (Mary Ann) 125.00
EGYPT — 8" straight leg, #543, 1986–1989 (Wendy Ann) 65.00
EGYPTIAN — 7–8" compo., 1936–1940 (Tiny Betty) 325.00
    9" compo., 1936–1940 (Little Betty) 375.00
ELAINE — 18" h.p., 1954 only, Me and My Shadow Series, blue organdy dress (Cissy) 1,500.00
    8" h.p., #0035E, 1954 only, matches 18" (Wendy Ann) . . . . .1,000.00 up
ELISE — 16½" h.p./vinyl arms (18", 1963 only), 1957–1964, jointed ankles & knees, good face color
    In street clothes or blouse, slacks & sash . . . . .350.00 up
    In ballgown, formal, or Portrait . . . . .700.00 up
    In riding habit, 1963 (Marybel head) 400.00
    Ballerina, rare yellow tutu, red hair 700.00
    With Marybel head, 1962 only 400.00
    18", 1963 only, with bouffant hairstyle 400.00
    17" h.p./vinyl, 1961–1962, one-piece arms & legs, jointed ankles & knees 275.00

17" ELISE, 1963, #1710. All original.

8" EASTER, 1953. Straight leg non-walker. Carries a basket with a chicken inside.

FLORA MCFLIMSEY, CONTINUED . . .

    15" Miss Flora McFlimsey, vinyl head (must have good color), 1953 only (Cissy) 600.00

    14", #25502, 1995, tiers of pink, white, and black, Button & Bows Series (Mary Ann) 135.00

FLOWERGIRL — 16"–18" compo., 1939, 1944–1947 (Princess Elizabeth) 550.00

    20–24" compo., 1939, 1944–1947 (Princess Elizabeth) ....650.00 up

    15–18" h.p., 1954 only (Cissy) 450.00–650.00

    15" h.p., 1954 only (Margaret) 550.00

    8" h.p., #602, 1956 (Wendy Ann) ....900.00 up

    8" h.p., #334, 1992–1993, Americana Series, white doll (Wendy Ann) 70.00

    8", #334-1, 1992 only, black doll 65.00

    10", #1122, 1988–1990, Portrette, pink dotted Swiss dress (Cissette) 85.00

FRANCE — 7" compo., 1936–1943 (Tiny Betty) 300.00

    9" compo., 1937–1941 (Little Betty) 325.00

    8" h.p., BKW, #390, #790, 1961–1965 (Wendy Ann) 125.00

    8" h.p., BK, #790, 1965–1972 ....100.00

    8" h.p., straight leg, #0790, #590, 1973–1975, marked "Alex." 75.00

    8" straight leg, #590, #552, #517, #582, 1976–1993, marked "Alexander" (1985–1987 white face) 60.00

    1985–1987, #590, #552, white face 55.00

    8" h.p., reissued 1994–1995, #110538 (Wendy Ann) 55.00

    8" h.p., #11557, 1996 International, cancan costume 70.00

FRENCH ARISTOCRAT — 10" Portrette, #1143, 1991–1992 only, bright pink/white (Cissette) 100.00

FRENCH FLOWERGIRL — 8" h.p., #610, 1956 only (Wendy Ann) ....750.00 up

FRIAR TUCK — 8" h.p., #493, 1989–1991, Storybook Series (Maggie Mixup) 75.00

FRIEDRICH — (see Sound of Music)

FROU-FROU — 40" all cloth, 1951 only, ballerina with yarn hair, dressed in green or lilac ....800.00 up

FUNNY — 18" cloth, 1963–1977 ....70.00

FUNNY MAGGIE — 8" (Maggie) #140506, 1994–1995, Storyland Series, yarn hair 55.00

8" FIRST COMMUNION, 1957, #395. Bend knee walker. All original.

8" FRANCE, 1985–87. Straight leg non-walker. Hard plastic.

Please read "What is a Price Guide?" for additional information.

GAINSBOROUGH — 20" h.p., 1957, Models Formal Gowns Series, taffeta gown, large picture hat (Cissy) . . .1,400.00 up
 #2184, 21" h.p./vinyl arms, 1968, blue with white lace jacket (Jacqueline) 650.00
 #2192, 21", 1972, yellow with full white lace overskirt (Jacqueline) 600.00
 #2192, 21", 1973, pale blue, scallop lace overskirt (Jacqueline) 550.00
 #2211, 21", 1978, pink with full lace overdress (Jacqueline) 425.00
 10" pink gown & hat, 1957 Portrette (Cissette) 600.00
 10", #45201, 1995, pink with lace overlay, Madame's Portfolio Series 110.00
GARDEN PARTY — 18" h.p., 1953 only (Margaret) 1,500.00
 20" h.p., 1956–1957 (Cissy) . . . . .1,000.00 up
 8" h.p., #488, 1955 only (Wendy Ann) . . . . .1,800.00 up
GARFIELD, LUCRETIA — 1985–1987, 4th set Presidents' Ladies/First Ladies Series (Louisa) 115.00
GENIUS BABY — 21"–30" plastic/vinyl, 1960–1961, has flirty eyes 150.00–250.00
 Little, 8" h.p. head/vinyl, 1956–1962 (see Little Genius)
GEPETTO — 8", #478, 1993, #140478, 1994, Storybook Series 70.00
GERANIUM — 9" early vinyl toddler, 1953 only, red organdy dress & bonnet 125.00
GERMAN (GERMANY) — 8" h.p., BK, #763, 1966–1972 (Wendy Ann) 100.00
 8" h.p., straight leg, #0763-563, 1973–1975, marked "Alex." 75.00
 10" h.p., 1962–1963 (Cissette) 975.00
 8" straight legs, #563, #535, #506, 1976–1989, marked "Alexander" (1985–1987 white face) 65.00
 8", 1990–1991, marked "Alexander" 60.00
 8", #535, 1986, white face 50.00
 8" h.p., #110542, 1994–1995, outfit in 1994 Neiman-Marcus trunk set (Maggie) 50.00

14" GIGI, 1986–1987. Classic Series.

10" GODEY, 1970, #1183. Hard plastic, Cissette, all original.

GET WELL WISHES — #10363–10365, 1995, 3 hair colors, nurse with bear, Special Occasions Series 60.00

GHOST OF CHRISTMAS PAST — 8", #18002, 1996, Dickens, long white gown 60.00

GHOST OF CHRISTMAS PRESENT — 14", #18406, 1996, Dickens, sold as set only with 8" Ignorance (boy)
and 8" Want (girl) 325.00

GIBSON GIRL — 10" h.p., 1962, eyeshadow (Cissette) 800.00

    1963, plain blouse with no stripes 800.00

    16" cloth, 1930's 850.00

    10", #1124, 1988–1990, Portrette, red and black (Cissette) 75.00

GIDGET — 14" plastic/vinyl, #1415, #1420, #1421, 1966 only (Mary Ann) 275.00

GIGI — 14", #1597, 1986–1987, Classic Series (Mary Ann) 95.00

    14", #87011, 1996, plaid dress, straw hat (Mary Ann) 125.00

GILBERT — 8", #260420, 1994–1995, Anne Green Gables Series 75.00

GIRL ON FLYING TRAPEZE — 40" cloth, 1951 only, dressed in pink satin tutu (sold at FAO Schwarz) 950.00

GLAMOUR GIRLS — 18" h.p., 1953 only (Margaret, Maggie) . . . . .1,400.00 up

GLINDA, THE GOOD WITCH — 8", #473, 1992–1993, Storyland Series (Wendy Ann) #140473, 1994-1995 . . . .85.00

    14" plastic/vinyl, #141573, 1994 only 100.00

    10", #13250, 1997, pink tulle and taffeta dress 115.00

GLORIOUS ANGEL — 10½" h.p., #54860 (see Tree Toppers)

GODEY — 21" compo., 1945–1947 (Wendy Ann) white lace over pink satin 2,700.00

    14" h.p., 1950–1951 (Margaret) 1,500.00

    21" h.p., 1951 only, lace ¾ top with long sleeves, pink satin two-tiered skirt (Margaret) . . . . . . .1,800.00 up

    18" h.p., #2010A, 1953 only, Glamour Girl Series, red gown with gray fur stole (Maggie) 1,500.00

    21" h.p., vinyl straight arms, 1961 only, lavender coat & hat (Cissy) 1,500.00

    21", #2153, 1965, dressed in all red, blonde hair (Jacqueline) 800.00

    21" plastic/vinyl, 1966 only, red with black short jacket & hat (Coco) 2,300.00

    21" h.p., vinyl arms, #2172, 1967, dressed in pink & ecru (Jacqueline) 650.00

    #2195, 1969, red with black trim 600.00

    #2195, 1970, pink with burgundy short jacket 375.00

    #2161, 1971, pink, black trim, short jacket 425.00

    #2298, 1977, ecru with red jacket and bonnet 350.00

    8" SLW, #491, 1955 only (Wendy Ann) . . . . .1,400.00 up

    10" h.p., #1172, 1968, dressed in all pink with ecru lace with bows down front (Cissette) 425.00

      #1172, 1969, all yellow with bows down front 450.00

      #1183, 1970, all lace pink dress with natural straw hat 425.00

GODEY BRIDE — 14" h.p., 1950, lace ¾ top over satin gown with long train (Margaret) . . . . .1,000.00 up

    18" h.p., 1950–1951 (Margaret) 1,100.00

    21" porcelain, 1993 (Cissy) 525.00

GODEY GROOM/MAN — 14" h.p., 1950, has curls over ears, wearing black jacket and tan pants (Margaret) 975.00

    18" h.p., 1950–1951 (Margaret) . . . . .1,200.00 up

GODEY LADY — 14" h.p., 1950, green velvet dress with pink/bright orange pleated ruffles,
peach/white bodice (Margaret) 950.00

    18" h.p., 1950–1951 (Margaret) 1,500.00

GOLDFISH — 8" h.p., #344, Americana Series 1993–1994 . . . . .80.00

GOLD RUSH — 10" h.p., 1963 only (Cissette) 1,600.00

GOLDILOCKS — 18" cloth, 1930's . . . . .875.00 up

    7–8" compo., 1938–1942 (Tiny Betty) 300.00

    18" h.p., 1951 only (Maggie) . . . . .1,300.00 up

    14" plastic/vinyl, #1520, 1978–1979, Classic Series, satin dress (Mary Ann) 115.00

    14", #1520, 1980–1983, blue satin or cotton dress (Mary Ann) 100.00

    14", #1553, 1991 only, Classic Series, long side curls tied with ribbon (Mary Ann) 100.00

    8", #497, 1990–1991 only, Storyland Series (1991 dress in different plaid) (Wendy Ann) 75.00

    8", #140500, 1994–1995, Storyland Series, floral print dress, has bear 65.00

GONE WITH THE WIND (SCARLETT) — 14", #1490, #1590, 1969–1986, all white dress/green sash,
made 17 years without a change (Mary Ann) (dress must be mint) . . . . .150.00 up

GOOD FAIRY — 14" h.p., 1948–1949 (Margaret) . . . . .725.00 up

GOOD LITTLE GIRL — 16" cloth, 1966 only, mate to "Bad Little Girl," wears pink dress 150.00

GOYA — 8" h.p., #314, 1953 only (Wendy Ann) ....1,000.00 up
    21" h.p./vinyl arms, #2183, 1968, multi-tiered pink dress (Jacqueline) 550.00
    21", #2235, 1982–1983, maroon dress with black Spanish lace (Jacqueline) 300.00
GRADUATION — 8" h.p., #399, 1957 only (Wendy Ann) ....800.00 up
    12", 1957 only (Lissy) 800.00
    8", #307, 1990–1991, Americana Series (white doll only) (Wendy Ann) 75.00
    8", #307, #307-1, 1991–1992, Americana Series, white or black doll 65.00
    8", #10307–10309 (black), #10310 (white), 1995, blue robe, Special Occasions Series 65.00
GRAND OLE OPRY BOY — 8", #77005, 1996 Classic 80.00
GRAND OLE OPRY GIRL — 8", #77004, 1996 Classic 80.00
GRANDMA JANE — 14" plastic/vinyl, #1420, 1970–1972 (Mary Ann) 275.00
GRANT, JULIA — 1982–1984, 3rd set Presidents' Ladies/First Ladies Series (Louisa) 125.00
GRAVE, ALICE — 18" cloth, 1930s ....750.00 up
GRAYSON, KATHRYN — 20–21" h.p., 1949 only (Margaret) ....5,500.00 up
GREAT BRITAIN — 8" h.p., #558, 1977–1988 (1985–1987 white face) (Wendy Ann) 60.00
GREAT GATSBY PAIR — 10", #15310, 1997, classic characters 180.00
GREECE BOY — 8" h.p., #527, 1992–1993 only (Wendy Ann) 55.00
GREEK BOY — 8" h.p., BK, 1965, & BKW, 1966–1968, #769 (Wendy Ann) 375.00
GREEK GIRL — 8" h.p., BK, #765, 1968–1972 (Wendy Ann) 100.00
    8" h.p., straight leg, #0765, #565, 1973–1975, marked "Alex" 75.00
    8" h.p., straight leg, #565, #527, 1976–1987 (1985–1987 white face), marked "Alexander" 55.00
GRETEL — 7" compo., 1935–1942 (Tiny Betty) 275.00
    9" compo., 1938–1940 (Little Betty) 325.00
    18" h.p., 1948 only (Margaret) ....1,000.00 up
    7½–8" h.p., SLW, #470, 1955 (Wendy Ann) ....400.00 up
    8" h.p., BK, #754, 1966–1972, Storybook Series (Wendy Ann) 90.00
    8" h.p., straight leg, #0754, #454, 1973–1975, marked "Alex" 75.00
    8" h.p., straight leg, #454, 1976–1986 (1986 white face), marked "Alexander" 65.00
    8" h.p., #462, 1991–1992 only, Storyland Series, reintroduced doll (Wendy Ann) 55.00
GRETEL BRINKER — 12", 1993 only (Lissy) 100.00
    8", #14650, 1996 ....57.00
GRETL — (see Sound of Music)
GROOM — 18"–21" compo., 1946–1947, mint (Margaret) 975.00
    18–21" h.p., 1949–1951 (Margaret) ....850.00 up
    14–16" h.p., 1949–1951 (Margaret) ....750.00 up
    7½" h.p., SL & SLW, #577, #464, #466, 1953–1955 (Wendy Ann) ....475.00 up
    8" BK, #577, 1956 ....375.00
    8" BK, #377, 1957 ....400.00
    8" BK, #572, 1958 ....375.00
      8" h.p., BK, #421, #442, 1961–1963 (Wendy Ann) 350.00
    8", #488, #388, reintroduced 1989–1991 only (Wendy Ann) 70.00
    8", #339, 1993, only black pants, peach tie, white jacket 70.00
    8", #17020, 1996, black velvet tails, black pants, pink tie 65.00
    8", #17023, 1996, black velvet tails, etc., black doll 65.00
    8", #21071, 1997, velvet tailcoat 58.00
GUARDIAN ANGEL — 10", #10602–1995, first in series, 100th Anniversary Special, all pink with white wings .125.00
    10", of Harmony, #10691, 1996 ....100.00
    10", of Hope, #10609, 1996 ....105.00
    10", of Love, frosted ivy, #10605, 1996 ....100.00
    10", of Love, heather blue #10607, 1996 ....100.00
    10", of Love, misty rose, #10603, 1996 ....100.00
    10", pink pristine, #10700, 1997, pink tulle dress 105.00
GUINEVERE — 10", #1146, 1992 only, Portrette, forest green/gold 125.00

Please read "What is a Price Guide?" for additional information.

HALLOWEEN WITCH — 8" (see Collectors United under Special Events/Exclusives) 100.00
HAMLET — 12", Romance Series (Nancy Drew) 90.00
    12", 1993 only (Lissy) 100.00
HANS BRINKER — 12", 1993 only (Lissy) 100.00
    8", #14649, 1996 . . . . .52.00
HANSEL — 7" compo., 1935–1942 (Tiny Betty) 300.00
    9" compo., 1938–1940 (Little Betty) 350.00
    18" h.p., 1948 only (Margaret) . . . . .800.00 up
    8" h.p., SLW, #470, 1955 only (Wendy Ann) . . . . .550.00 up
    8" h.p., BK, #753, 1966–1972, Storybook Series (Wendy Ann) 100.00
    8" h.p., straight leg, #0753, #543, 1973–1975, marked "Alex." 75.00
    8" h.p., straight leg, #543, 1976–1986 (1986 white face), marked "Alexander" 60.00
    8" h.p., #461, 1991–1992 only, Storyland Series, reintroduced doll (Wendy Ann) 55.00
HAPPY — 20" cloth/vinyl, 1970 only 225.00
HAPPY BIRTHDAY — 1985 (see M.A.D.C. under Special Events/Exclusives) 325.00
    8" h.p., #325, #325-1, 1992–1993, Americana Series, black or white doll (Wendy Ann) 65.00
    8" h.p., #100325, 1994, white only 60.00
    8", #10325–10327, 1995, three hair colors, Special Occasions Series 65.00
    8", #17004–17010, 1996, three hair colors, black or white doll (Wendy, Maggie) 60.00
    14" plastic/vinyl, #241596, 1994 only 100.00
HAPPY BIRTHDAY BILLIE — 8" h.p., #345, #345-1, Americana Series, black or white boy, 1993 only 65.00
HAPPY BIRTHDAY MAGGIE — 8", #21080 – white, #21083 – black, 1997 .58.00
HAPPY CHANUKAH — 8", #10367, 1996 Holiday, #19630, 1997 . . . . .65.00
HAPPY THE CLOWN — 8", #10414, 1996 Classic Circus 55.00
HARDING, FLORENCE — 1988, 5th set Presidents' Ladies/First Ladies Series (Louisa) 125.00
HARLEQUIN — 8", #14574, 1995, Nutcracker Series 65.00
HARLEY DAVIDSON
    8", h.p., #77002, 1996 (Wendy) Classic American, #17420, 1997 . . . . .100.00
    8", h.p., #77005, 1996 (Billy) Classic American, #17410, 1997 . . . . .100.00
    10", h.p. #77102, 1996, pictured 1996 catalog . . . . .Not Available for Sale
    10", #17440, 1997, Cissette, black leather coat, boots 125.00
    10", #17430, 1997, David, jeans, black leather jacket 125.00
HARRISON, CAROLINE — 1985–1987, 4th set Presidents' Ladies/First Ladies Series (Louisa) 125.00
HAWAII — 8", #301, 1990–1991 only, Americana Series, (Wendy Ann) 75.00
HAWAIIAN — 8" h.p., BK, #722, 1966–1969, Americana Series (Wendy Ann) 375.00
    7" compo., 1936–1939 (Tiny Betty) 300.00
    9" compo., 1937–1944 (Little Betty) 350.00
HAYES, LUCY — 1985–1987, 4th set Presidents' Ladies/First Ladies Series (Louisa) 125.00
HEATHER — 18" cloth/vinyl, 1990 only 100.00

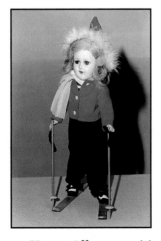

SONJA HENIE. All composition.

HEIDI — 7" compo., 1938–1939 (Tiny Betty) 300.00
    8" h.p., #460, 1991–1992, Storyland Series (Maggie) 70.00
    14" plastic/vinyl, #1480, #1580, #1581, 1969–1985 (16 year production), Classic Series (Mary Ann) 85.00
    14", #1581, 1986–1988, solid green dress, floral apron 85.00
    14", #25503, 1995, Ribbons & Bows Series (not on order sheet) . . . . Not Available
HELLO BABY — 22", 1962 only 175.00
HENIE, SONJA — 13–15" compo., 1939–1942 . . . . .600.00
    7" compo., 1939–1942 (Tiny Betty) 425.00
    9" compo., 1940–1941 (Little Betty) 575.00
    11" compo. (Wendy Ann) 550.00
    14" compo. 675.00
    14" in case/wardrobe . . . . .1,800.00 up
    17–18" compo. 950.00
    20–23" compo. 1,200.00
    13–14" compo., jointed waist 750.00
    15–18" h.p./vinyl, 1951 only, no extra joints, must have good face color (Madeline) 750.00
HER FIRST DAY AT SCHOOL — (see Wendy Loves Series)
HER LADY AND CHILD (THUMBELINA) — 21" porcelain, 8" h.p., #010, 1992–1994, limited to 2,500 . . . . . .500.00
HER SUNDAY BEST — (see Wendy Loves Series)
HIAWATHA — 8" h.p., #720, 1967–1969, Americana Series (Wendy Ann) 375.00
    7" compo. (Tiny Betty) 300.00
    18" cloth, early 1930's 800.00
HIGHLAND FLING — 8" h.p., #484, 1955 only (Wendy Ann) 650.00
HOLIDAY ON ICE — 8" h.p., #319, 1992–1993 only, red with white fur hat and muff,
    some tagged Christmas on Ice 100.00
HOLLAND — 7" compo., 1936–1943 (Tiny Betty) 300.00
HOLLY — 10", #1135, 1990–1991, Portrette, white/red roses (Cissette) 100.00
HOLLYWOOD TRUNK SET — 8", #15340, 1997 . . . . .250.00
HOMECOMING — 8", 1993 (see M.A.D.C. under Special Events/Exclusives) 200.00
HOME FOR HOLIDAYS — 14", #24606, 1995, Christmas Series 105.00
HONEYBEA — 12" vinyl, 1963 only 175.00
HONEYETTE BABY — 16" compo./cloth, 1941–1942 . . . . .225.00
    7" compo., 1934–1937, little girl dress (Tiny Betty) 275.00
HONEYBUN — 18–19", 1951–1952 only 200.00
    23–26" 300.00
HONEYMOON IN NEW ORLEANS — 8" (see Scarlett)
HOOVER, LOU — 14", 1989–1990, 6th set Presidents' Ladies/First Ladies Series (Mary Ann) 125.00
HOPE — 8" (see Collectors United under Special Events/Exclusives) 175.00
HUCKLEBERRY FINN — 8" h.p., #490, 1989–1991 only, Storybook Series (Wendy Ann) 80.00
HUG ME PETS — #76001–76007, plush animal bodies, huggums face 58.00
HUGGUMS, BIG — 25", 1963–1979, boy or girl 100.00
HUGGUMS, LITTLE — 14", 1986 only, molded hair 50.00
    12", 1963–1995, molded hair, available in 7–10 outfits (first black version available in 1995) 50.00
    12", 1963–1982, 1988, rooted hair 40.00
    1991, special outfits (see Imaginarium Shop under Special Events/Exclusives) 60.00
    1996–1997, variety of outfits . . . . .40.00 up
HUGGUMS, LIVELY — 25", 1963 only, knob makes limbs and head move 150.00
HUGGUMS MAN IN THE MOON MOBILE — #14700, 8" boy, star costume, cloth moon, star mobiles 60.00
HULDA — 18" h.p., 1949 only, lamb's wool wig black doll (Margaret) . . . . .1,900.00 up
    14" h.p., 1948–1949, lamb's wool wig, black doll . . . . .1,275.00 up
HUMPTY DUMPTY — 8", #13060, 1997, plaid tailcoat, brick wall 70.00
HUNGARIAN (HUNGARY) — 8" h.p., BKW, #397, #797, 1962–1965 (Wendy Ann) 135.00
    BK, #397, with metal crown 125.00
    BK, #797, 1965–1972 . . . . .100.00
    8" h.p., straight leg, #0797, #597, 1973–1976, marked "Alex." 70.00
    8" h.p., straight leg, #597, 1976–1986 (1986 white face), marked "Alexander" 60.00
    8" h.p., #522, reintroduced 1992–1993 only (Wendy Ann) 55.00
    8", #11547, 1995 only 60.00
HYACINTH — 9" early vinyl toddler, 1953 only, blue dress & bonnet 150.00

Please read "What is a Price Guide?" for additional information.

IBIZA — 8", #510, 1989 only (Wendy Ann) 80.00
ICE CAPADES — 1950's (Cissy) . . . . .1,400.00 up
    1960's (Jacqueline) . . . . .1,600.00 up
ICE SKATER — 8" h.p., BK & BKW, #555, 1955–1956 (Wendy Ann) . . . . .700.00 up
    8", #303, 1990–1991 only, Americana Series, purple/silver (Wendy Ann) 75.00
    8", #16371, 1997, boy, brocade vest, black pants 58.00
    8", #16361, 1997, girl, pink knit and silver outfit 58.00
ICELAND — 10", 1962–1963 (Cissette) . . . . .750.00 up
IGNORANCE — 8", #18406 (see Ghost of Christmas Present) (sold as set)
I LOVE YOU — 8", #10386–10388, 1995, three hair colors, Special Occasions Series 60.00
I. MAGNIN — (see Special Events/Exclusives)
IMAGINARIUM SHOP — (see Special Events/Exclusives)
INDIA — 8" h.p., BKW, #775, 1965 (Wendy Ann) 175.00
    8" h.p., BK, #775, 1965–1972 (Wendy Ann) 100.00
    8" h.p., #775, BK & BKW, white . . . . .100.00 up
    8" h.p., straight leg, #0775, #575, 1973–1975, marked "Alex." 70.00
    8" h.p., straight leg, #575, #549, 1976–1988, marked "Alexander" (1985–1987 white face) 60.00
    8" h.p., straight leg, #11563, 1996 International, #24030, 1997 . . . . .65.00
INDIAN BOY* — 8" h.p., BK, #720, 1966 only, Americana Series (Wendy Ann) 500.00
INDIAN GIRL* — 8" h.p., BK, #721, 1966 only, Americana Series (Wendy Ann) 500.00
INDONESIA — 8" h.p., BK, #779, 1970–1972 (Wendy Ann) 100.00
    8" h.p., straight leg, #779, #0779, #579, 1972–1975, marked "Alex." 75.00
    8" h.p., straight leg, #579, 1976–1988, marked "Alexander" 60.00
    8" BK, with Maggie Mixup face 175.00
INGALLS, LAURA — 14", #1531, 1989–1991, Classic Series, burnt orange dress/blue pinafore (Mary Ann) 90.00
    14", #24621, 1995, green with rose floral, Favorite Books Series (Mary Ann) 105.00
INGRES — 14" plastic/vinyl, #1567, 1987 only, Fine Arts Series (Mary Ann) 90.00
IRIS — 10" h.p., #1112, 1987–1988, pale blue (Cissette) 90.00
IRISH (IRELAND) — 8" h.p., BKW, #778, 1965 only (Wendy Ann) .125.00
    8" BK, #778, 1966–1972, long gown 100.00
    8" straight leg, #0778, #578, 1973–1975, marked "ALEX," long gown 75.00
    8" straight leg, #578, #551, 1976–1985, marked "Alexander" 65.00
    8" straight leg, #551, 1985–1987, short dress, white face 60.00
    8" straight leg, #551, 1987–1993, marked "Alexander," short dress (Maggie) 55.00
    8" h.p., #100541, re-issued 1994 only, green skirt with white top 55.00
    8" h.p., #17028, 1996 International, Leprechaun outfit, #21000, 1997 . . . . .60.00
IRISH LASS — 8", #11555, 1995 only 60.00
ISOLDE — 14", #1413, 1985–1986 only, Opera Series (Mary Ann) 90.00
ISRAEL — 8" h.p., BK, #768, 1965–1972 (Wendy Ann) 100.00
    8" h.p., straight leg, #0768, 1973–1975, marked "Alex." 75.00
    8" h.p., straight leg, #568, 1976–1989 (1985–1987 white face), marked "Alexander" 65.00
ITALY — 8" h.p., BKW, #393, 1961–1965 (Wendy Ann) 125.00
    8" h.p., BK, #793, 1965–1972 . . . . .100.00
    8" h.p., straight leg, #0793, #593, 1973–1975, marked "ALEX." .70.00
    #593, 1985, white face 60.00
    8" straight leg, #593, #553, #524, 1976–1994 (#110524), marked "Alexander" 65.00
    8", #11549, 1995 only 60.00
    8", #24050, 1997, gondolier outfit, with decorated oar 68.00

* BECAME HIAWATHA AND POCAHONTAS IN 1967.

J

Please read "What is a Price Guide?" for additional information.

JACK & JILL — 7" compo., 1938–1943 (Tiny Betty) . . . . 275.00 each
   9" compo., 1939 only (Little Betty) . . . . 325.00 each
   8" straight leg (Jack - #455, #457. Jill - #456, #458), 1987–1992, Storybook Series (Maggie) . . . . 65.00 each
   8" straight leg, sold as set, #14626, 1996 (Wendy Ann) 105.00
JACK BE NIMBLE — 8" (see Dolly Dears under Special Events/Exclusives) 125.00
JACKIE — 10", #45200, 1995, Madame's Portfolio Series, pink suit 80.00
   10" h.p., #20115, 1996, wedding gown, Classic American 105.00
   21", #17450, 1997, 3 outfits, 3 pieces luggage, jewelry, etc. 630.00
   10", #17460, 1997, pink luncheon suit 105.00
JACKIE AND JOHN — 10", #20117, 1996, limited edition . . . . .210.00 set
JACKSON, SARAH — 1979–1981, 2nd set Presidents' Ladies/First Ladies Series (Louisa) 125.00
JACQUELINE IN RIDING HABIT — 21" h.p./vinyl arms, 1961–1962, street dress or suit, pillbox hat . . . . . . .800.00 up
   In sheath dress and hat or slacks and top 650.00
   In gown from cover of 1962 catalog 950.00
   Ballgown other than 1962 catalog cover 850.00
   10" h.p., 1962 only (Cissette) 650.00
JACQUELINE — 1962, 1966–1967, exclusive in trunk with wardrobe . . . . .1,800.00 up
JAMAICA — 8" straight leg, #542, 1986–1988 (Wendy Ann) 80.00
JANIE — 12" toddler, #1156, 1964–1966 only 275.00
   Ballerina, 1965 only 350.00
   14" baby, 1972–1973 . . . . .65.00
   20" baby, 1972–1973 . . . . .85.00
JAPAN — 8" h.p., BK, #770, 1968–1972 (Wendy Ann) 100.00
   8" h.p., straight leg, #0770, #570, 1973–1975, marked "Alex" .75.00
   8" h.p., straight leg, #570, 1976–1986, marked "Alexander" 55.00
   8", #570, 1987–1991 (Maggie) 55.00
   8" BK, #770, 1960s (Maggie Mixup) 200.00
   8" h.p., #526, reintroduced 1992–1993 only, white face (Wendy Ann) 60.00
JASMINE — 10", #1113, 1987–1988, Portrette, burnt orange (Cissette), 1997 . . . . .130.00

**10" JACQUELINE, 1962, #885. Hard plastic, Cissette. Pink satin
ball gown with evening bag, pearl necklace, and earrings.**

JEANNIE WALKER — 13–14" compo., 1940's, unique jointed legs, excellent face color, mint condition . . .675.00 up

18" compo., 1940's . . . . .700.00 up

JENNIFER'S TRUNK SET — 14" doll, #1599, 1990 only 250.00

JESSICA — 18" cloth/vinyl, 1990 only 150.00

JINGLES THE JUGGLER — 8", #10404, 1996, jester's outfit 65.00

JO — (see Little Women)

JO GOES TO NEW YORK — 8", #14522, 1995 only, trunk set using Meg doll, Little Women Series . . . . . .200.00 set

JOANIE — 36" plastic/vinyl, 1960–1961, allow more for flirty eyes

36", 1960, nurse dressed in all white with black band on cap .475.00 up

36", 1961, nurse in colored uniform, all white pinafore and cap . . . . .425.00 up

JOHN — 8", #440, 1993 only, Peter Pan Series, wears glasses 70.00

JOHN POWERS MODELS — 14" h.p., 1952 only, must be mint (Maggie & Margaret) . . . . .1,650.00 up

18", 1952 only . . . . .1,900.00 up

JONES, CASEY — 8" h.p., Americana Series, 1991–1992 only (Wendy Ann) 60.00

JOHNSON, LADY BIRD — 14", 1994 only 125.00

JOLLY OLD SAINT NICK — 16", #19620, 1997 . . . . .190.00

JOSEPH, THE DREAM TELLER — 8", #14580, 1995 only, Bible Series 75.00

JOSEPHINE — 12", #1335, 1980–1986, Portraits of History (Nancy Drew) 75.00

21" Portrait, 1994 only 350.00

JOY — 12", (see New England Collectors Society under Special Events/Exclusives) 225.00

JOY NOEL — 8" (see Spiegel's under Special Events/Exclusives) 125.00

JUDY — 21" compo., 1945–1947, pinch pleated flowers at hem (Wendy Ann) . . . . .3,200.00 up

21" h.p./vinyl arms, 1962 only (Jacqueline) . . . . .1,850.00 up

JUGO-SLAV — 7" compo., 1935–1937 (Tiny Betty) 225.00

JULIET — 21" compo., 1945–1946, Portrait (Wendy Ann) . . . . .2,500.00 up

18" compo., 1937–1940 (Wendy Ann) . . . . .1,275.00 up

8" h.p., #473, 1955 only (Wendy Ann) . . . . .950.00 up

12" plastic/vinyl, 1978–1987, Portrait Children Series (Nancy Drew) 65.00

12", reintroduced 1991–1992, Romance Collection (Nancy Drew) 85.00

8" (see Madame Alexander Doll Company under Specials Events/Exclusives) 125.00

JUNE BRIDE — 21" compo., 1939, 1946–1947, Portrait Series, embroidered flowers near hem

(Wendy Ann) . . . . .2,500.00 up

JUNE WEDDING — 8" h.p., 1956 . . . . .600.00

JOHN POWERS MODEL, 1952 only.
Hard plastic, "Maggie" face.

Please read "What is a Price Guide?" for additional information.

KAREN — 15–18" h.p., 1948–1949 (Margaret) . . . . .750.00 up
KAREN BALLERINA — 15" compo., 1946–1949 (Margaret) . . . . .850.00 up
   18" compo., 1948–1949 (Margaret) . . . . .1,200.00 up
   18–21", h.p., can be dressed in pink, yellow, blue, white, or lavender . . . . .950.00 up
KATE GREENAWAY — 7" compo., 1938–1943 (Tiny Betty) 325.00
   9" compo., 1936–1939 (Little Betty) 375.00
   16" cloth, 1936–1938 . . . . .900.00
   13", 14", 15" compo., 1938–1943 (Princess Elizabeth) 750.00
   18", 1938–1943 (Wendy Ann/Princess Elizabeth) 800.00
   24", 1938–1943 (Princess Elizabeth) . . . . .900.00 up
   14" vinyl, #1538, 1993 only, Classic Series 100.00
KATHLEEN TODDLER — 23" rigid vinyl, 1959 only 150.00
KATHY — 17"–21" compo., 1939, 1946 (Wendy Ann) 650.00–850.00
   15–18" h.p., 1949–1951, has braids (Maggie) 550.00–700.00
KATHY BABY — 13–15" vinyl, 1954–1956, has rooted or molded hair 75.00–125.00
   11–13" vinyl, 1955–1956, has rooted or molded hair 75.00–125.00
   18–21", 1954–1956, has rooted or molded hair 100.00–150.00
   11" vinyl, 1955–1956, doll has molded hair and comes with trousseau 175.00
   21", 1954 only 150.00
   21" & 25", 1955–1956 . . . . .100.00–175.00
KATHY CRY DOLLY — 11–15" vinyl nurser, 1957–1958 . . . . .75.00–125.00
   18", 21", 25" 100.00–175.00
KATHY TEARS — 11", 15", 17" vinyl, 1959–1962, has closed mouth .75.00–125.00
   19", 23", 26", 1959–1962 . . . . .100.00–175.00
   12", 16", 19" vinyl, 1960–1961 (new face) 75.00–125.00
KATIE (BLACK SMARTY) — 12" plastic/vinyl, 1963 only 325.00
   12" (black Janie), #1156, #1155, 1965 only 300.00
   12" h.p., 1962, 100th Anniversary doll for FAO Schwarz (Lissy) .1,000.00 up
KEANE, DORIS — Cloth, 1930's 750.00
   9–11" compo., 1936–1937 (Little Betty) 250.00–300.00
KELLY — 12" h.p., 1959 only (Lissy) 450.00
   15–16", 1958–1959 (Marybel) 300.00
   16", 1959 only, in trunk/wardrobe . . . . .800.00 up
   18", 1958 . . . . .375.00
   22", 1958–1959 . . . . .400.00
   8" h.p., #433, 1959, blue/white dress 575.00
KELLY BLUE DOT GINGHAM — 18", #29100, 1997, vinyl 125.00
KELLY HAPPY BIRTHDAY — 18", #29230, 1997, vinyl 125.00
KELLY PINK DOT TULLE — 18", #29230, 1997, vinyl 125.00
KELLY PINK SNOWFLAKE — 18", #29110, 1997, vinyl 125.00
KELLY TREE TRIMMING — 18", #29240, 1997, vinyl 125.00
KENNEDY, JACQUELINE — 14", 1989–1990, 6th set Presidents' Ladies/First Ladies Series (Mary Ann) 175.00
KENYA — 8", 1994, outfit tagged, in Neiman-Marcus trunk set
   8", issued 1995 only, same outfit but sold as **NIGERIA** . . . . No Price Available
KING — 21" compo., 1942–1946 , extra makeup, red chest ribbon, gold trimmed cape (Wendy Ann) . 2,700.00 up
KING OF HEARTS — 8", #14611, 1996, Alice in Wonderland series 62.00
KITTEN — 14–18" cloth/vinyl, 1962–1963 . . . . .50.00–85.00
   24", 1961 only, has rooted hair 95.00
   20" nurser, 1968 only, has cryer box, doesn't wet 90.00
   20", 1985–1986 only, dressed in pink 90.00
KITTY BABY — 21" compo., 1941–1942 . . . . .175.00
KITTEN KRIES — 20" cloth/vinyl, 1967 only 100.00
KITTEN, LITTLEST — (see Littlest Kitten)

KITTEN, LIVELY — 14", 18", 24", 1962–1963, knob moves head and limbs .100.00–175.00

KITTEN, MAMA — 18", #402, 1963 only, same as "Lively" but also has cryer box 140.00

KLONDIKE KATE — 10" h.p., 1963 only, Portrette (Cissette) . . . . .1,400.00 up

KNAVE — 8", #13040, 1997, brocade suit, large playing card, *5 of Spades* 75.00

KOREA — 8" h.p., BK, #772, 1968–1970 (Wendy Ann) 175.00

    BKW & BK, #772, (Maggie Mixup) 225.00

    #522, reintroduced 1988–1989 (Maggie Mixup) 75.00

KULDA — 8", #11101, 1995 only, International Folk Tales (Russia) (Wendy Ann) 60.00

KWANZAA CELEBRATION — 10" h.p., #10368, 1996 Holiday 95.00

22" KELLYS, 1959. "Marybel" face. All original clothing.

Please read "What is a Price Guide?" for additional information.

LADY AND HER CHILD — 21" porcelain, 8" h.p., 1993 ....500.00 set
LADY BIRD — 8", #438, 1988–1989, Storybook Series (Maggie) 85.00
LADY HAMILTON — 20" h.p./vinyl arms, 1957 only, Models Formal Gowns Series, picture hat, blue gown w/
    shoulder shawl effect (Cissy) ....850.00 up
        11" h.p., 1957, pink silk gown, picture hat with roses (Cissette) ....600.00 up
        21", #2182, 1968, beige lace over pink gown (Jacqueline) 475.00
        12" vinyl, #1338, 1984–1986, Portraits of History (Nancy Drew) 75.00
LADY IN RED — 20", #1134, 1958 only, red taffeta (Cissy) ....1,800.00 up
    10", 1990, Portrette (Cissette) 90.00
LADY IN WAITING — 8" h.p., #487, 1955 only (Wendy Ann) ....1,400.00 up
LADY LEE — 8", #442, 1988 only, Storybook Series 70.00
LADY LOVELACE — Cloth/felt, 1930's 650.00
LADY VALENTINE — 8" #140503, 1994 only (Wendy Ann) 65.00
LADY WINDERMERE — 21" compo., 1945–1946, extra makeup, Portrait Series ....2,500.00 up
LANCELOT — 8", #79529, 1995, 100th Anniversary (copy of 1995 Disney auction doll) 100.00
LANE, HARRIET — 1982–1984, 3rd set Presidents' Ladies/First Ladies Series (Mary Ann) 125.00
LAOS — 8" straight leg, #525, 1987–1988 ....70.00
LAPLAND — 8" h.p., #537, 1993 ....65.00
LASSIE — 8", #11102, 1995 only, International Folk Tales (Norway) 60.00
LATVIA — 8" straight leg, #527, 1987 only 75.00
LAUGHING ALLEGRA — Cloth, 1932 ....650.00
LAURIE, LITTLE MEN — 8" h.p., BK, #781, #755, 1966–1972 (Wendy Ann) 175.00
    Straight leg, #0755, #416, 1973–1975, marked "Alex." 100.00
    Check pants, marked "Alexander" 85.00
    Straight leg, #416, #410, 1976–1992 (1985–1987 white face) 65.00
    8", #14620, 1996, waistcoat, houndstooth trousers 60.00
    12" all h.p., 1966 only (Lissy) 500.00
    12" plastic/vinyl, 1967–1988 (Nancy Drew) 65.00

21" Coco, 1966, #2051. Lissy Portrait. A very rare doll.

LAURIE with the Lissy face, 1967, #1226. All hard plastic. Rare.

LAURIE, PIPER — 14" h.p., 1950 only (Margaret) . . . . .2,400.00 up
   21" h.p., 1950 only (Margaret) . . . . .2,900.00 up
LAZY MARY — 7" compo., 1936–1938 (Tiny Betty) 250.00
LENA (RIVERBOAT QUEEN) — (see M.A.D.C. under Special Events/Exclusives) 300.00
LENNOX, MARY, — 14" Classic Series, 1993–1994 . . . . .100.00
LE PETIT BOUDOIR — 1993 (see Collectors United under Special Events/Exclusives) 100.00
LESLIE (BLACK POLLY) — 17" vinyl, 1965–1971, in dress 275.00
   1966–1971, as bride 300.00
   1965–1971, in formal or ballgown 300.00
   In trunk with wardrobe . . . . .650.00 up
   1966–1971, as ballerina 375.00
LETTY BRIDESMAID — 7–8" compo., 1938–1940 (Tiny Betty) 275.00
LEWIS, SHARI — 14", 1958–1959 . . . . .650.00
   21", 1958–1959 . . . . .850.00
LIBERACE WITH CANDELABRA — 8", #22080, 1997, velvet cape 115.00
LIESL — (see Sound of Music)
'LIL CHRISTMAS CANDY — 8" h.p.,#100348, 1994 only, Americana Series 65.00
'LIL CHRISTMAS COOKIE — 8", #341, 1993–1994, Americana Series 65.00
'LIL CLARA AND THE NUTCRACKER — 8", #140480, 1994, Storyland Series 65.00
'LIL SIR GENIUS — 7", #701 & #400701 vinyl, painted eyes, 1993, in blue jumpsuit 50.00
LILA BRIDESMAID — 7–8" compo., 1938–1940 (Tiny Betty) 300.00
LILAC FAIRIE — 21" , 1993, Portrait ballerina 300.00
LILIBET — 16" compo., 1938 (Princess Elizabeth) . . . . .750.00 up
LILY — 10", #1114, 1987–1988, red/black (Cissette) 85.00
LINCOLN, MARY TODD — 1982–1984, 3rd set Presidents' Ladies/First Ladies Series (Louisa) 150.00
LIND, JENNY — 21" h.p./vinyl arms, #2191, 1969, dressed in all pink, no trim (Jacqueline) 1,400.00
   #2181, 1970, all pink with lace trim 1,500.00
   10", #1171, 1969, Portrette, all pink, no trim (Cissette) 600.00
   10", #1184, 1970, Portrette, pink with lace trim (Cissette) 650.00

8" LITTLE VICTORIA, 1953–54 only. Matches larger Binne walker dolls.

8" LITTLE GENIUS, 1961, #217. Vinyl. Candy stripe dress and bonnet with original spoon.

LIND, JENNY, CONTINUED . . .

14" plastic/vinyl, #1491, 1970 only, Portrait Children Series (Mary Ann) pink, lace trim 375.00
LIND, JENNY & LISTENING CAT — 14", #1470, 1969–1971, Portrait Children Series, blue dot dress apron &
holds plush kitten (must have kitten) (Mary Ann) 275.00
LION TAMER — 8", #306, 1990, Americana Series (Wendy Ann) 70.00
LISSY — 11½"–12" h.p., 1956–1958, jointed knees & elbows
   1956–1958, as ballerina 375.00
   1956–1958, as bride . . . . .375.00 up
   1956–1957, as bridesmaid . . . . .450.00 up
   1958, dressed in formal . . . . .500.00 up
   1956–1958, in street dresses 350.00
   1956, in window box with wardrobe . . . . .1,300.00 up
   21", one-piece arm, pink tulle pleated skirt (Cissy) 1,250.00
   21", #2051, 1966, pink with tiara (Coco) 2,200.00
   12" h.p., 1957, jointed elbows & knees, in window box with wardrobe (Lissy) . . . . . .1,200.00 up
   12" h.p., one-piece arms & legs in window box/wardrobe, 1959–1966 (Lissy) . . . . . .1,200.00 up
   Classics (see individuals, example: McGuffey Ana, Scarlett, Cinderella)
LITHUANIA — 8" h.p., #110544, 1994 only (Wendy Ann) 60.00
LITTLE ANGEL — 9" latex/vinyl, 1950–1957 . . . . .200.00
LITTLE AUDREY — Vinyl, 1954 only . . . . .475.00 up
LITTLE BETTY — 9–11" compo., 1935–1943, must be mint 250.00–300.00
LITTLE BITSEY — 9" all vinyl nurser, 1967–1968 (Sweet Tears) 150.00
LITTLE BO PEEP — (see Bo Peep, Little)
LITTLE BOY BLUE — 7" compo., 1937–1939 (Tiny Betty) 300.00
LITTLE BUTCH — 9" all vinyl nurser, 1967–1968 (Sweet Tears) 150.00
LITTLE CHERUB — 11" compo., 1945–1946 . . . . .275.00
   7" all vinyl, 1960 only 250.00
LITTLE CHRISTMAS PRINCESS — 8", #10369, 1996 Holiday 65.00
LITTLE COLONEL — 8½–9" compo. (*rare size*), 1935, closed mouth (Betty) 650.00
   11–13" compo. (*rare size*), closed mouth (Betty) 550.00–650.00
   17" compo., closed mouth (Betty) . . . . .750.00 up
   14", open mouth (Betty) 650.00
   17"–23", open mouth 750.00–950.00
   26–27", open mouth . . . . .1,250.00 up
LITTLE DEVIL — 8" h.p., Americana Series, 1992–1993 only 60.00
LITTLE DORRIT — 16" cloth, early 1930's, Dickens character 700.00
LITTLE EDWARDIAN — 8" h.p., SL, SLW, #0200, 1953–1955, long dotted navy gown . . . . .950.00 up
LITTLE EMILY — 16" cloth, early 1930's, Dickens character 650.00
LITTLE EMPEROR — 8" (see U.F.D.C. under Special Events/Exclusives) 500.00
LITTLE GENIUS — 12–14" compo./cloth, 1935–1940, 1942–1946 . . . . .200.00
   16–20" compo./cloth, 1935–1937, 1942–1946 . . . . .250.00
   24–25", 1936–1940 . . . . .150.00
   8" h.p./vinyl, 1956–1962, nude (clean condition), good face color 100.00
     Dressed in cotton play dress 175.00
     In dressy, lacy outfit with bonnet 275.00
     Dressed in christening outfit 300.00
   Sewing or Gift Set, 1950's . . . . .850.00 up
   7" vinyl, 1993–1995, reintroduced doll with painted eyes 50.00
     #701 & 400701, 1993–1995, dressed in blue jumpsuit (Lil' Sir Genius) 50.00
     #702 & 400702, 1993–1995, dressed in pink lacy dress (Lil' Miss Genius) 55.00
     1993, extra packaged outfits . . . . .30.00 each
     Christening Baby, #400703, 1994-1995 . . . . .50.00
     Super Genius, #400704, 1994–1995, dressed in Superman style outfit 50.00
     Birthday Party, #400705, 1994 only 50.00
     Genius Elf, #400706, 1994–1995, dressed in Christmas red and green 50.00

LITTLE GODEY — 8" h.p., #491, 1953–1955 (Wendy Ann) ....1,100.00 up

LITTLE GRANNY — 14" plastic/vinyl, #1431, 1966 only, floral gown (Mary Ann) 250.00

    14", #1430, 1966 only, pinstriped gown (also variations) (Mary Ann) 225.00

LITTLE HUGGUMS — (see Huggums)

LITTLE JACK HORNER — 7" compo., 1937–1943 (Tiny Betty) 300.00

LITTLE JUMPING JOAN — 8", #487, 1989–1990, Storybook Series (Maggie Mixup) 75.00

LITTLE LADY DOLL — 8" h.p., #1050, 1960 only, gift set in mint condition (Maggie Mixup) ....750.00 up

    8" doll only, must have correct hairdo and excellent face color 350.00

    21" h.p., 1949, has braids & colonial gown, extra makeup, Portrait Series (Wendy Ann) 2,400.00

LITTLE LORD FAUNTLEROY — Cloth, 1930's 750.00

    13" compo., 1936–1937 (Wendy Ann) ....650.00 up

LITTLE MADELINE — 8" h.p., 1953–1954 (Wendy Ann) ....700.00 up

LITTLE MAID — 8" straight leg, #423, 1987–1988, Storybook Series (Wendy Ann) 70.00

LITTLE MEN — 15" h.p., 1950–1952 (Margaret & Maggie) ....850.00 each

LITTLE MEN — Set with Tommy, Nat & Stuffy, must be in excellent condition ....2,600.00 set

LITTLE MERMAID — 10", #1145, 1992–1993, Portrette, green/blue outfit (Cissette) 115.00

    8", #14531, 1995, Hans Christian Andersen Series, has long black hair 60.00

LITTLE MINISTER — 8" h.p., #411, 1957 only (Wendy Ann) ....2,600.00 up

LITTLE MISS — 8" h.p., #489, 1989–1991 only, Storybook Series (Maggie Mixup) 75.00

LITTLE MISS GODEY — (see M.A.D.C. under Special Events/Exclusives) 150.00

LITTLE MISS MAGNIN — (see I. Magnin under Special Events/Exclusives) 150.00

LITTLE NANNIE ETTICOAT — #428, 1986–1988, straight leg, Storybook Series 80.00

LITTLE NELL — 16" cloth, early 1930's, Dickens character ....650.00 up

    14" compo., 1938–1940 (Wendy Ann) 675.00

LITTLE PRINCESS — 14", #26415, 1995 only, has trunk and wardrobe (Louisa) 250.00

LITTLE SHAVER — 10" cloth, 1940–1944 ....450.00 up

    7" cloth, 1940–1944 ....550.00

    15" cloth, 1940–1944 ....600.00

    22" cloth, 1940–1944 ....650.00 up

    12" cloth, 1941–1943 (see Baby Shaver)

    12" plastic/vinyl, 1963–1965, has painted eyes 250.00

LITTLE SOUTHERN BOY/GIRL — 10" latex/vinyl, 1950–1951 ....150.00 each

LITTLE SOUTHERN GIRL — 8" h.p., #305, 1953 only (Wendy Ann) ....950.00 up

LITTLE THUMBKINS — 8", #14532, Hans Christian Andersen Series, lavender/pink/yellow tiers 65.00

LITTLE VICTORIA — 7½"–8", #376, 1953–1954 only (Wendy Ann) ....1,200.00 up

LITTLE WOMEN — Meg, Jo, Amy, Beth (Marme/Marmee in sets when available)

    16" cloth, 1930–1936 ....700.00 up each

    7" compo., 1935–1944 (Tiny Betty) ....300.00 each

    9" compo., 1937–1940 (Little Betty) ....300.00 each

    13–15" compo., 1937–1946 (Wendy Ann) ....325.00 each

    14–15" h.p., 1947–1956, plus Marme (Margaret & Maggie) ....450.00 each ....2,200.00 set

    14"–15" h.p., widespread fingers, ca. 1949–1952 ....475.00 each

    14–15" h.p., BK, plus Marme (Margaret & Maggie) ....450.00 each .....2,200.00 set

    14–15" Amy with loop curls, must have good face color (Margaret) ....500.00 each

    8" Amy with loop curls, 1991 #411 ....85.00 each

    7½–8" h.p., SL, SLW, all #609, 1955, plus Marme (Wendy Ann) ......375.00 each .....1,800.00 set

    8" h.p., BKW, all #609, all #409, all #481, 1956–1959 (Wendy Ann) ...250.00 each .....1,300.00 set

    8" BK, all #381, 1960–1963, (Wendy Ann) ....150.00 each ......750.00 set

        #781, 1964–1971 ....125.00 each ......650.00 set

        #7811 to #7815, 1972–1973 ....100.00 each ......650.00 set

    8" straight leg, #411 to #415, 1974–1986 ....75.00 each ....375.00 set

        #405 to #409, 1987–1990 ....65.00 each ....375.00 set

        #411 to #415, 1991–1992 ....65.00 each ....375.00 set

        #14523–14528, 1995 ....60.00 each ....325.00 set

        Exclusive for FAO Schwarz (see Special Events/Exclusives) ....125.00 each ......750.00 set

LITTLE WOMEN, CONTINUED . . .

10", #14630–14633, 1996 . . . . .82.00 each . . . . . . .350.00 set
11½–12" h.p., jointed elbows & knees, 1957–1958 (Lissy) . . . . 375.00 each . . . . .1,900.00 set
11½–12" h.p., one-piece arms & legs, 1959–1968 (Lissy) . . . . 250.00 each . . . . .1,200.00 set
12" plastic/vinyl, 1969–1982 (Nancy Drew) . . . . 65.00 each . . . . . . .350.00 set
12" plastic/vinyl, 1983–1989, new outfits (Nancy Drew) . . . . 70.00 each . . . . . . .375.00 set
12", 1989–1990 only (see Sears unders Special Events/Exclusives) . . . . .450.00 set
12", 1993 only, no Marme (Lissy) . . . . 100.00 each
16", 1997, plastic/vinyl, Little Women Journal Series .105.00 each
LITTLEST KITTEN — 8" vinyl, 1963, nude, clean, good face color . . . . .125.00 up
    Dressed in lacy dress oufit with bonnet . . . . .300.00 up
    Dressed in christening outfit . . . . .325.00 up
    In sewing or gift set . . . . .700.00 up
    Dressed in play attire 175.00
LIVELY HUGGUMS — 25", knob makes limbs and head move, 1963 . . . . .150.00
LIVELY KITTEN — 14", 18", 24", 1962–1963, knob makes limbs and head move 125.00–175.00
LIVELY PUSSY CAT — 14", 20", 24", 1966–1969, knob makes limbs and head move 125.00–175.00
LOLA AND LOLLIE BRIDESMAID — 7" compo., 1938–1940 (Tiny Betty) . . . . 300.00 up each
LOLLIE BABY — Rubber/compo, 1941–1942 . . . . .100.00
LOLLIPOP MUNCHKIN — (see Munchkin)
LOOBY LOO — 15½" h.p., ca. 1951–1954 . . . . .675.00 up
LORD FAUNTLEROY — 12", 1981–1983, Portrait Children (Nancy Drew) 85.00
LORD VALENTINE — 8" #140502, 1994 only (Wendy Ann) 65.00
LOUISA — (see Sound of Music)
LOVE — 8" (see Collectors United under Specials Events/Exclusives) 95.00
    8", made for public in 1994 (Only differences on C.U. doll are gold locket, pearls set into cap, and
        gold metal braids on slippers, heart box) 75.00
LOVEY DOVE (DOVEY) — 19" vinyl baby, 1958–1959, closed mouth, molded or rooted hair, few are mistagged . .150.00
    19" h.p./latex, 1950–1951 . . . . .100.00
    12" all h.p. toddler, 1948–1951 (Precious) . . . . .375.00 up
    1951, dressed as "Ringbearer" . . . . .600.00 up
    "Answer Doll" with lever in back to move head . . . . .525.00 up
LUCINDA — 12" plastic/vinyl, 1969–1970 (Janie) . . . . .350.00 up
    14" plastic/vinyl, #1435, #1535, 1971–1982 (11 year production), blue gown (Mary Ann) 90.00
    14", #1535, 1983–1986, Classic Series, pink or peach gown (Mary Ann) 90.00
LUCK OF THE IRISH — 8", #327, 1992–1993 only, Americana Series (Maggie Mixup) 60.00
LUCY — 8" h.p., #488, 1961 only, Americana Series, strip cotton/poke bonnet (Wendy Ann) . . . . . . .1,500.00 up
LUCY BRIDE — 14" h.p., 1949–1950 (Margaret) 600.00
    17" h.p., 1949–1950 (Margaret) 625.00
    16½" h.p./vinyl arms, 1958 only (Elise) 450.00
    14" compo., 1937–1940 (Wendy Ann) 450.00
    17" compo., 1937–1940 (Wendy Ann) 550.00
    21" compo., 1942–1944, Portrait, extra make-up (Wendy Ann) 2,500.00
LUCY LOCKET — 8" straight leg, #433, 1986–1988, Storybook Series 85.00
    14", #25501, 1995, Ribbons & Bows Series, purple floral skirt (Louisa) 160.00
LUCY RICARDO — (see FAO Schwarz under Special Events/Exclusives) 150.00
    9", '50s gingham dress, with bottle and spoon 115.00
    21", #50003, 1996 Timeless Legends, black dress with black and white polka dots accents 325.00
LUCY AND RICKY — 9" set, Vitameatavegamin episode 200.00
LULLABY MUNCHKIN — (see Munchkin)

Please read "What is a Price Guide?" for additional information.

MAD HATTER — 8", #14510, 1995, Alice in Wonderland Series 65.00
M.A.D.C. (MADAME ALEXANDER DOLL CLUB) — (see Special Events/Exclusives)
MADAME BUTTERFLY — 10" (see Marshall Fields under Special Events/Exclusives) 125.00
    8", h.p., #22000, 1997, shadow, kimono 95.00
    21", #22010, 1997, kimono over silk robe 350.00
MADAME DOLL — 21" h.p./vinyl arms, 1966 only, pink brocade (Coco) . . . . .2,200.00 up
    14" plastic/vinyl, #1460, #1561, 1967–1975, Classic Series (Mary Ann) 200.00
MADAME (ALEXANDER) — 21", 1984 only, one-piece skirt in pink 400.00
    21", 1985–1987, pink with overskirt that unsnaps 325.00
    21", 1988–1990, blue with full lace overskirt 325.00
    21", #79507, 1995, 100th Anniversary, pink with lace jacket, limited edition of 500 . . . . .750.00
    8", 1993 only, introduced mid-year (see Madame Alexander Doll Co. under Special Events/Exclusives) . . .125.00
    8" in blue gown (see Doll & Teddy Bear Expo. under Special Events/Exclusives) 275.00
    8", #79527, 1995, 100th Anniversary 100.00
MADAME ALEXANDER COLLECTOR'S PHONOGRAPH ALBUM —1978, Madame's voice reading children's stories . . .35.00
MADAME POMPADOUR — 21" h.p./vinyl arms, #2197, 1970, pink lace overskirt (Jacqueline) 1,200.00
MADELAINE — 14" compo., 1940–1942 (Wendy Ann) 600.00
    8" h.p., 1954, FAO Schwarz special . . . . .800.00 up
MADELAINE DU BAIN — 11" compo., closed mouth, 1937 (Wendy Ann) .500.00
    14" compo., 1938–1939 (Wendy Ann) 525.00
    17" compo., 1939–1941 (Wendy Ann) 650.00
    21" compo., 1939–1941 (Wendy Ann) 900.00
    14" h.p., 1949–1951 (Maggie) . . . . .950.00 up
MADELINE — 17–18" h.p./jointed elbows & knees, 1950–1953 . . . . .800.00 up
    18" h.p., 1961 only, vinyl head, extra jointed body, wears short dress, must be mint . . . . .700.00 up
        Ballgown 1961 only . . . . .800.00 up
MADISON, DOLLY — 1976–1978, 1st set Presidents' Ladies/First Ladies Series (Martha) 125.00
MADONNA AND CHILD — 10", #10600, 1995, Christmas Series 105.00
MAGGIE — 15" h.p., 1948–1954 (Little Women only to 1956) 550.00

10" MARGOT, 1961, #925. White satin gown and coat. "Cissette" face. Mint and all original.

MARGOT BALLERINA, 1954, #1550. Hard plastic, "Margaret" face. Mint and all original.

MAGGIE, CONTINUED . . .

17–18", 1949–1953	.650.00
20–21", 1948–1954	.700.00
22–23", 1949–1952	.800.00
17" plastic/vinyl, 1972–1973 only (Elise)	.175.00

MAGGIE ELF — 8", #14585, 1995, Christmas Series 65.00

MAGGIE MIXUP — 16½" h.p./vinyl, 1960 only (Elise body) 375.00

17" plastic/vinyl, 1961 only	.400.00 up
8" h.p., #600, #611, #617, #627, 1960–1961, freckles	.475.00 up
8" Wendy Ann face, freckles	.500.00
8" h.p., #618, 1961, as angel	.750.00
8", #610, 1960–1961, dressed in overalls and has watering can	.700.00
8", #626, 1960–1961, dressed in skater outfit	.700.00 up
8", #634, 1960–1961, dressed in riding habit	.550.00
8", #593, 1960, dressed in roller skating outfit	.750.00
8", #598, #597, #596, 1960, wearing dresses or skirts/blouses	.450.00 up
8", #31000, 1997, Post Office commemorative, blue gingham	.75.00

MAGGIE TEENAGER — 15–18" h.p., 1951–1953 ... .475.00–600.00 up

23", 1951–1953	.650.00 up

MAGGIE WALKER — 15–18" h.p., 1949–1953 ... .400.00–575.00

20–21", 1949–1953	.575.00
23–25", 1951–1953 (with Cissy face)	.650.00

MAGNOLIA — 21", #2297, 1977 only, many rows of lace on pink gown 500.00

21", #2251, 1988 only, yellow gown	.325.00

MAID MARIAN — 8" h.p., #492, 1989–1991 only, Storybook Series (Wendy Ann) 100.00

21", 1992–1993 only, Portrait Series (Jacqueline)	.325.00

MAID OF HONOR — 18" compo., 1940–1944 (Wendy Ann) ... .700.00 up

14" plastic/vinyl, #1592, 1988–1989, Classic Series, blue gown (Mary Ann)	.90.00

MAJORETTE — 14–17" compo., 1937–1938 (Wendy Ann) ... .850.00 up

DRUM MAJORETTE — 8" h.p., #482, 1955 only, (Wendy Ann)	.950.00 up
8", #314, 1991–1992 only, Americana Series, no baton	.65.00

20" McGUFFEY ANA. All composition. Mint with original box.

MALI — 8", #11565, 1996 International, African-American print costume 60.00
MAMBO — 8", h.p., #481, 1955 only (Wendy Ann) . . . . .700.00 up
MAMMY — 8", #402, 1989 only, Jubilee II set (black "round" face) 100.00
    8" h.p., #635, 1991–1992 only, Scarlett Series (black Wendy Ann) 85.00
    10" h.p., #15010, 1997 (black Wendy Ann) 95.00
MANET — 21", #2225, 1982–1983, light brown with dark brown pinstripes (Jacqueline) 275.00
    14", #1571, 1986–1987, Fine Arts Series (Mary Ann) 85.00
MARCELLA DOLLS — 13–24" compo., 1936 only, dressed in 1930's fashions . . . . .650.00–900.00 each
MARCH HARE — Cloth/felt, mid 1930's 675.00
MARGARET (O'BRIEN) — 14" h.p., nude with excellent color . . . . .250.00   18" 550.00
    14" h.p. in tagged Alexander boxed clothes .475.00   18" 650.00
    21" compo., tagged Alexander clothes . . . . .900.00 up
MARGARET ROSE — (see Princess Margaret Rose)
MARGOT — 10–11" h.p., 1961 only, in formals (Cissette) . . . . .450.00 up
    Street dresses, bathing suit, 1961 only 350.00
MARGOT BALLERINA — 15–18", 1953–1955, dressed in various colored outfits (Margaret & Maggie) . .675.00–750.00
    15–18" h.p./vinyl arms, 1955 only (Cissy) 375.00–475.00
MARIA — (see Sound of Music)
MARIE ANTOINETTE — 21", #2248, 1987–1988, multi-floral print with pink front insert (Jacqueline) 425.00
    21" compo., 1944–1946, Portrait with extra makeup and in mint condition (Wendy Ann) 2,100.00
MARILLA — 10", #261-168, 1994, Anne of Green Gables Series 85.00
MARINE — 14" compo., 1943–1944 (Wendy Ann as boy) 800.00
MARIONETTES/TONY SARG — 12–14" compo., 1934–1940 . . . . .400.00
    12" compo., Disney Characters 400.00
MARLEY'S GHOST — 8", #18004, 1996, Dickens, silver chains 60.00
MARM LIZA — 21" compo., 1938 and 1946, extra makeup, mint condition (Wendy Ann) 3,200.00
MARME — (see Little Women)
MARSHALL FIELDS — (see Special Events/Exclusives)
MARTA — (see Sound of Music)
MARTIN, MARY — 14–17" h.p., 1948–1952, wearing jumpsuit (Margaret) 700.00–875.00
    14–17", 1948–1952, dressed in sailor suit or ballgown (Nell from *South Pacific*) 800.00–975.00

Original box for McGuffey Ana.

MARY, JOSEPH, BABY JESUS IN MANGER — 8", #19470, 1997, Nativity set .190.00
MARY ANN — 14" plastic/vinyl, 1965, tagged "Mary Ann", in red/white dress 275.00
    Dressed in skirt and sweater 250.00
    Ballerina 250.00
    14" ballerina, 1973–1982 . . . . .150.00
    14", reintroduced #241599, 1994 only 75.00
MARYBEL "THE DOLL THAT GETS WELL" — 16" rigid vinyl, 1959–1965, doll only . . . . .200.00 up
    1959, 1961, 1965, doll in case 375.00
    1960 only, doll in case with wardrobe 400.00
    1965 only, doll with very long straight hair, in case 450.00
MARY CASSATT BABY — 14" cloth/vinyl, 1969–1970 . . . . .175.00
    20", 1969–1970 . . . . .250.00
    14" plastic/vinyl child, #1566, 1987 only, Fine Arts Series (Mary Ann) 85.00
MARY ELLEN — 31" rigid vinyl, walker, 1954 only . . . . .600.00 up
    31" plastic/vinyl arms, 1955 only, non-walker with jointed elbows . . . . .500.00 up
MARY ELLEN PLAYMATE — 16" plastic/vinyl, 1965 only, Marshall Fields exclusive (Mary Ann) 325.00
    12", 1965, in case with wigs (Lissy) . . . . .700.00 up
    17", 1965, exclusive 350.00
MARY GRAY — 14" plastic/vinyl, #1564, 1988 only, Classic Series (Mary Ann) 85.00
MARY HAD A LITTLE LAMB — 8", #14623, 1996 Nursery Rhyme, #11610, 1997 . . . . .65.00
MARY LENNOX — 14", #1537, 1993–1994, Classic Doll Series 95.00
MARY LOUISE — 21" compo., 1938, 1946–1947, golden brown/burnt orange (Wendy Ann) 2,700.00
    18" h.p., 1954 only, Me & My Shadow Series, burnt orange & olive green (Cissy) 1,250.00
    8" h.p., #0035D, 1954 only, same as 18", Me & My Shadow Series (Wendy Ann) . . . . .1,200.00 up
MARY, MARY — 8" h.p., BKW, BK, #751, 1965–1972, Storybook Series (Wendy Ann) 125.00
    8" h.p., straight leg, #0751, #451, 1973–1975, marked "Alex" .75.00
    8" h.p., straight leg, #451, 1976–1987, marked "Alexander" (1985–1987 white face) 65.00
    8", #471, reintroduced 1992 only (Wendy Ann) 60.00
    8", #14556, 1996, floral dress, straw hat, #11600, 1997 . . . . .65.00
    14", #1569, 1988–1991, Classic Series (Mary Ann) 80.00
    14", #241595, reintroduced 1994 only 100.00

**MAGGIE MIXUP ANGEL COSTUME, 1961, #0618.
Mint in original box.**

MARY MINE — 21" cloth/vinyl, 1977–1989 ....125.00
    14" cloth/vinyl, 1977–1979 ....100.00
    14", reintroduced 1989 ....65.00
MARY MUSLIN — 19" cloth, 1951 only, pansy eyes 500.00
    26", 1951 only 575.00
    40", 1951 only 850.00
MARY, QUEEN OF SCOTS — 21", #2252, 1988–1989 (Jacqueline) 350.00
MARY ROSE BRIDE — 17" h.p., 1951 only (Margaret) ....600.00 up
MARY SUNSHINE, LITTLE — 15" plastic/vinyl, 1961 (Caroline) 375.00
MARZIPAN DANCER — 10", #14573, 1995, Nutcracker Series (Cissette) 75.00
MATTHEW — 8", #26424, 1995, Anne of Green Gables Series 60.00
MCELROY, MARY — 1985–1987, 4th set Presidents' Ladies/First Ladies Series (Mary Ann) ...125.00
MCGUFFEY ANA — 16" cloth, 1934–1936 ....675.00
    7" compo., 1935–1939 (Tiny Betty) 375.00
    9" compo., 1935–1939 (Little Betty) 400.00
    15" compo., 1935–1937 (Betty) 650.00
    13" compo., 1938 (Wendy Ann) 650.00
    11", 1937–1939, has closed mouth 675.00
    11–13" compo., 1937–1944 (Princess Elizabeth) 575.00
    14–16" compo., 1937–1944 (Princess Elizabeth) 600.00
    17–20" compo., 1937–1943 (Princess Elizabeth) 675.00–850.00
    21–25" compo., 1937–1942 (Princess Elizabeth) ..750.00–1,000.00
    28" compo., 1937–1939 (Princess Elizabeth) 1,200.00
    17" compo., 1948–1949 (Margaret) 800.00
    14½" compo., 1948, wears coat, hat & muff 950.00
    18", 25", 31", 1955–1956, has flat feet (Cissy) ..500.00–950.00
    21" h.p., 1948–1950 (Margaret) 1,200.00
    12" h.p. (*rare doll),* 1963 only (Lissy) ....1,700.00 up
    8" h.p., #616, 1956 only (Wendy Ann) 750.00
    8" h.p., #788, #388, 1963–1965 (was "American Girl" in 1962–1963) 375.00
    8", #496, 1990–1991 only, Storybook Series (Wendy Ann) 75.00
    29" cloth/vinyl, 1952 only (Barbara Jane) 650.00
MCGUFFEY ANA
    14" plastic/vinyl, #1450, 1968–1969, Classic Series, wears plaid dress/eyelet apron (Mary Ann) 120.00
    14" plastic/vinyl, #1525, 1977–1986, Classic Series, wears plaid dress (Mary Ann) 85.00
    14" plastic/vinyl, #1526, 1987–1988, mauve stripe pinafore, Classic Series (Mary Ann) 85.00
    14", #24622, 1995, red plaid dress, Nostalgia Series (Mary Ann) 90.00
MCKEE, MARY — 1985–1987, 4th set Presidents' Ladies/First Ladies Series (Mary Ann) 125.00
MCKINLEY, IDA — 1988, 5th set Presidents' Ladies/First Ladies Series (Louisa) 125.00
ME AND MY SCASSI — (see FAO Schwarz under Special Events/Exclusives) 375.00
MEDICI, CATHERINE DE — 21" porcelain, 1990–1991 ....500.00
MEG — 8", #79530, 100th Anniversary, two-tiered blue gown with white and rose trim 100.00
(also see Little Women)
MELANIE — 21" compo., 1945–1947 (Wendy Ann) ....2,300.00 up
    21" h.p./vinyl arms, 1961, lace bodice & overdress over satin (Cissy) ......975.00 up
    21", #2050, 1966, blue gown with wide lace down sides (Coco) ....2,200.00 up
    #2173, 1967, blue dress with white rick-rack around hem ruffle (Jacqueline) 675.00
    #2181, 1968, blue dress with white trim 525.00
    #2193, 1969, blue gown, white trim, many rows of lace, bonnet 550.00
    #2196, 1970, white gown with red ribbon trim 525.00
    #2162, 1971, blue gown, white sequin trim 450.00
    #2195, 1974, white gown, red jacket and bonnet 500.00
    #2220, 1979–1980, white dotted swiss gown with pink trim 350.00
        1981, pink nylon with blue ribbon 350.00
    #2254, 1989, all orange with lace shawl 350.00

9" McGuffey Ana, 1930's. Composition. Original box states Alexander Doll Co. Madame Alexander Creations, New York.

Melanie, continued . . .

10", #1173, 1968–1969, pink multi-tiered skirt (Cissette) 450.00
10", #1182, 1970, yellow multi-tiered skirt 475.00
8" h.p., #633, 1955–1956, green velvet (Wendy Ann) . . . . .1,000.00 up
12", 1987 only, Portrait Children Series, aqua green gown, brown trim (Nancy Drew) 80.00
10", #1101, 1989 only, Jubilee II, all royal blue dress with black trim (Cissette) 125.00
8", #627, 1990, Scarlett Series, lavender/lace (Wendy Ann) 90.00
8", #628, 1992, peach gown/bonnet with lace 75.00
10", #16555, 1996, Melanie's Sewing Circle, blue dress 95.00
Melinda — 10" h.p., 1968–1969, blue gown with white trim (Cissette) 450.00
10" h.p., 1970, yellow multi-tiered lace skirt 425.00
22", #1912, 1962 only, wears white organdy dress with red trim 375.00
14", 16", 22" plastic/vinyl, 1962–1963, cotton dress . . . . .300.00–375.00 up
14", 16", 22" plastic/vinyl, 1963, party dress 375.00–475.00
14", 1963 only, as ballerina 350.00
Melody and Friend — 25" and 8" (see Madame Alexander Doll Co. under Special Events/Exclusives) . . . .700.00 set
Merry Angel — 8", (see Spiegel's under Special Events/Exclusives) 150.00
Metroplex Doll Club — (see Special Events/Exclusives)
Mexico — 7" compo., 1936 (Tiny Betty) 275.00
9" compo., 1938–1939 (Little Betty) 300.00
8" h.p., BKW, #776, 1964–1965 (Wendy Ann) 125.00
8" h.p., BK, #776, 1965–1972 . . . . .100.00
8" straight leg, #0776, 1973–1975, marked "ALEX" 70.00
8" straight leg, #576, #550, #520, 1976–1991, marked "Alexander" (1985–1987 white face) 65.00
8", #11551, 1995 only (Maggie) 60.00
8", #24100, 1997, Mariachi outfit, guitar 75.00
Michael — 11" plastic/vinyl, 1969 only (Janie) (Peter Pan set) 375.00
With teddy bear, mint condition 425.00
8", #468, 1992–1993, Storybook Series (Peter Pan set) (Wendy Ann) .70.00

MIDNIGHT — 21", #2256, 1990, dark blue/black (Jacqueline) 325.00
MILLER'S DAUGHTER — 14" with 8" Rumpelstilskin, #1569, 1992 only, limited to 3,000 sets . . . . .275.00 set
MILLY 17" plastic/vinyl, 1968 only (Polly) 400.00
MIMI — 30", h.p. in 1961 only, multi-jointed body, dressed in formal 950.00
        Dressed in romper suit/skirt 550.00
MIMI
    Dressed in Tyrolean outfit 950.00
    Dressed in slacks, stripe top, straw hat 600.00
    Dressed in red sweater, plaid skirt 600.00
    21" h.p./vinyl arms, #2170, 1971, vivid pink cape & trim on white gown (Jacqueline) 500.00
    14", #1411, 1983–1986, Opera Series (Mary Ann) 90.00
MINISTER, LITTLE — 8" h.p., #411, 1957 only . . . . .2,600.00 up
MIRACLE SANTA — 10", 1996, with street sign 155.00
MIRACLE WENDY — 8", 1996 . . . . .172.00
MISS AMERICA — 14" compo., 1941–1943, holds flag . . . . .850.00 up
MISS ELIZA DOOLITTLE — 10", #20112, 1996 Classic 95.00
MISS GULCH WITH BICYCLE, TOTO — 10", #13240, 1997, Wizard of Oz Series 125.00
MISS LEIGH — 8", 1989, made for C.U. Gathering (see Special Events/Exclusives) 150.00
MISS LIBERTY — 10" (see M.A.D.C. under Special Events/Exclusives) 125.00
MISS MAGNIN — 10" (see I. Magnin under Special Events/Exclusives) 150.00
MISS MUFFETT, LITTLE — 8" h.p., BK, #752, 1965–1972, Storybook Series (Wendy Ann) 125.00
    8" straight leg, #0752, #452, 1973–1975, marked "Alex" 75.00
    8" straight leg, #452, 1976–1986 (1985–1986 white face), marked "Alexander" (Wendy Ann) 65.00
    8" straight leg, #452, 1987–1988 (Maggie) 65.00
    8", #493, 1993, Storybook Series #140493, 1994 . . . . .65.00
MISS SCARLETT — 14" (see Belk & Leggett under Special Events/Exclusives) 125.00
MISS UNITY — 10", (see U.F.D.C. under Special Events/Exclusives) 450.00
MISS U.S.A. — 8" h.p., BK, #728, 1966–1968, Americana Series (Wendy Ann) 325.00
MISS VICTORY — 20" compo., 1944–1946, magnets in hands (Princess Elizabeth) . . . . .750.00 up

MADELAINE DUBAIN, 1937–1941. All composition with human hair wig. Original clothing.

MISTERIOSO — 10" h.p., #20119, 1996 Cirque du Soleil Series 85.00
MISTRESS MARY — 7" compo., 1937–1941 (Tiny Betty) 300.00
MOLLY — 14", #1561, 1988 only, Classic Series (Mary Ann) 85.00
MOLLY COTTONTAIL — Cloth/felt, 1930's 625.00
MOMMY & ME — 14" and 7" compo., 1948–1949 (Margaret and Tiny Betty) . . . . .1,700.00 up set
MOMMY & ME ON-THE-GO — 8", 10", h.p., #11010, 1997 . . . . .160.00
MOMMY & ME AT HOME — 8", 10", h.p., #11009, 1997, pink floral outfits .160.00
MOMMY'S PET — 14–20", 1977–1986 . . . . .65.00–150.00 up
MONA LISA, DAVINCI'S — 8", h.p., 1997, #22140, green velvet dress 80.00
MONET — 21", #2245, 1984–1985, black & white check gown with red jacket (Jacqueline) 300.00
MONIQUE — 8", (see Disney under Specials Events/Exclusives) . . . . .600.00 up
MONROE, ELIZABETH — 1976–1978, 1st set Presidents' Ladies/First Ladies Series (Mary Ann) 150.00
MOP-TOP ANNIE — 8", #14486, 1995, red dress with white dots 65.00
MOP-TOP WENDY — 8" #140484, 1993–1995, Toy Shelf Series 65.00
MOP-TOP BILLY — 8" #140485, 1993–1995, Toy Shelf Series 65.00
MORISOT — 21", #2236, 1985–1986 only, lime green gown with white lace (Jacqueline) 275.00
MORNING GLORY — 14", #25505, Ribbons & Bows Series, floral dress with lace (Mary Ann) 155.00
MOROCCO — 8" h.p., BK, #762, 1968–1970 (Wendy Ann) 300.00
    8", h.p. #11559, 1996 International, belly dancer 65.00
MOSS ROSE — 14", #1559, 1991 only, Classic Series (Louisa) 150.00
MOTHER & ME — 14–15" and 9" compo., 1940–1943, mint condition (Wendy Ann & Little Betty) . . . .1,400.00 up
MOTHER GOOSE — 8" straight leg, #427, #459, 1986–1992, Storybook Series (Wendy Ann) 70.00
    8", #11620, 1997, with goose and book of rhymes 70.00
MOTHER GOTHEL AND RAPUNZEL — 8" & 14", #1539, 1993–1994, limited to 3,000 sets. . . . . 250.00 set
MOTHER HUBBARD — 8", #439, #459, 1988–1989, Storyland Series (Wendy Ann) 75.00
MOTHER'S DAY — 8", #10380–10382, 1995, three hair colors, Special Occasions 60.00
MOUSKETEER — 8" (see Disney under Special Events/Exclusives) 125.00
MR. AND MRS. FRANKENSTEIN SET — 8", 1996 . . . . .155.00
MR. O'HARA — 8", #638, 1993 only, Scarlett Series (Wendy Ann) 100.00
MRS. BUCK RABBIT — Cloth/felt, mid-1930's 625.00
MRS. CLAUS — (see mid-year specials for Madame Alexander Co. under Special Events/Exclusives) 75.00
    14", #24607, 1995, Christmas Series 100.00
MRS. DARLING — 10", 1993–1994, Peter Pan Series (Cissette) 125.00
MRS. FEZZIWIG — 8", #18005, 1996, Dickens, moiré gown 60.00
MRS. MARCH HARE — Cloth/felt, mid-1930's 625.00
MRS. MALLOY'S MILLINERY SHOP — 10" Portrette, #201167, 1995 only, trunk set with wardrobe and hats 225.00
MRS. O'HARA — 8", #638, 1992–1993 only, Scarlett Series (Wendy Ann) .100.00
MRS. QUACK-A-FIELD — Cloth/felt, mid-1930's 625.00
MRS. SNOOPIE — Cloth/felt, 1940's 625.00
MUFFIN — 19" cloth, 1966 only 125.00
    14", 1963–1977 . . . . .95.00
    14" cloth, 1965 only, sapphire eyes 95.00
    14" black cloth, 1965–1966 only 125.00
    14" cloth, 1966–1970, cut slanted blue eyes 100.00
    14" cloth, eyes like sideways commas 75.00
    12" all vinyl, 1989–1990 (Janie) 75.00
    12", 1990–1992, in trunk/wardrobe 150.00
MUNCHKIN PEASANT — 8", #140444, 1993–1995, Wizard of Oz Series 65.00
    HERALD — 8" #140445, 1994–1995, Wizard of Oz Series 75.00
    MAYOR — 8", #140443, 1993–1995, Wizard of Oz Series 65.00
    LOLLIPOP — 8", #14513, 1995, Wizard of Oz Series, pink/white striped outfit 65.00
    LULLABY — 8", #14512, 1995, Wizard of Oz Series, white gown 65.00
MY DOLL HOUSE — (see Special Events/Exclusives)
MY LITTLE SWEETHEART — (see Child At Heart under Special Events/Exclusives) 75.00

Please read "What is a Price Guide?" for additional information.

NAN McDARE — Cloth/felt, 1940's 625.00
NANA — 6" dog with bonnet, #441, 1993 only, Peter Pan Series 55.00
NANA/GOVERNESS — 8" h.p., #433, 1957 only (Wendy Ann) ....2,000.00 up
NANCY ANN — 17–18" h.p., 1950 only (tagged Nancy Ann) ....975.00 up
NANCY DAWSON — 8", #441, 1988–1989, Storybook Series (Maggie) 80.00
NANCY DREW — 12" plastic/vinyl, 1967 only, Literature Series ....350.00 up
NANCY JEAN — 8", (see Belks & Leggett under Special Events/Exclusives) 75.00
NAPOLEON — 12", #1330, 1980–1986, Portraits of History (Nancy Drew) 75.00
NAT (LITTLE MEN) — 15" h.p., 1952 (Maggie) ....900.00 up
NATASHA — 21", #2255, 1989–1990, brown & paisley brocade (Jacqueline) 350.00
NATIVITY SET — 1997, 19460, Mary, Joseph, Jesus, Angel creche, Three Wise Men, Shepherd, Drummer ...950.00
NASHVILLE GOES COUNTRY — 8" (1995, see C.U. under Special Events/Exclusives)
NASHVILLE SKATER — #1, (see Collectors United under Special Events/Exclusives) 175.00
    #2, (see Collectors United under Special Events/Exclusives) 95.00
NATIONAL VELVET — 12", 1991 only, Romance Series, no riding crop (Nancy Drew) 85.00
    8", #10409, 1996, riding habit 75.00
NEIMAN-MARCUS — (see Special Events/Exclusives)
NELSON, LORD — 12" vinyl, 1336, 1984–1986, Portraits of History (Nancy Drew) 75.00
NETHERLANDS BOY — Formerly "Dutch" (Wendy Ann)
    8" h.p., straight leg, #577, 1974–1975, marked "Alex" 75.00
    8" h.p., straight leg, #577, 1976–1989, marked "Alexander" (1985–1987 white face) ...65.00
NETHERLANDS GIRL — 8" h.p., #591, #525, 1974–1992 (Wendy Ann) 60.00
NEW ENGLAND COLLECTOR SOCIETY — (see Special Events/Exclusives)
NICOLE — 10", #1139, 1989–1990, Portrette, black/off white outfit (Cissette) 90.00
NIGERIA — 8", #11552, 1995 only (also in 1994 Neiman-Marcus trunk set as KENYA) 60.00

**14" NINA BALLERINA, 1949–51. Hard plastic,
"Margaret" face.**

NIGHTINGALE, FLORENCE — 14", #1598, 1986–1987, Classic Series 85.00
NINA BALLERINA — 7" compo., 1940 (Tiny Betty) 325.00
   9" compo., 1939–1941 (Little Betty) 350.00
   14" h.p., 1949–1951 (Margaret) . . . . .550.00 up
   17", 1949–1951 . . . . .550.00
   15" h.p., 1951, came in various colors all years (Margaret) 700.00
   19", 1949–1950 . . . . .850.00 up
   23", 1951 . . . . .800.00
NIXON, PAT — 14", 1994 only (see Presidents' Ladies/First Ladies Series) 135.00
NOD — (see Dutch Lullaby)
NOEL — 12" (see New England Collector Society under Special Events/Exclusives) 250.00
NORMANDY — 7" compo., 1935–1938 (Tiny Betty) 275.00
NORWAY — 8" h.p., BK, #584, 1968–1972 (Wendy Ann) 100.00
   8" straight leg, #584, 1973–1975, marked "Alex." 75.00
   8" straight leg, #584, 1976–1987, marked "Alexander" (1985–1987 white face) 65.00
   8" straight leg, #11566, 1996 International Viking costume 75.00
NORWEGIAN — 7–8" compo., 1936–1940 (Tiny Betty) 300.00
   9" compo., 1938–1939 (Little Betty) 325.00
NURSE — 16", 1930's, cloth and felt 675.00
   7" compo., 1937, 1941–1943 (Tiny Betty) 275.00
   9" compo., 1939, 1942–1943 . . . . .325.00
   13–15" compo., 1936–1937 (Betty) all white outfit, Dionne nurse . . . . . . MIB – 900.00 up . . . . . .700.00 up
   15" compo., 1939, 1943 (Princess Elizabeth) 500.00
   14" h.p., 1948 (Maggie & Margaret) 850.00
   8" h.p., #563, 1956 only, all white dress (Wendy Ann) . . . . .650.00 up
   8", #429, 1961, all white dress, comes with baby . . . . .650.00 up
   8" BKW, BK, #329, #460, #660, #624, 1962–1965, wears stripe dress, comes with baby 475.00
   8", #308, all white uniform, Americana Series, 1991 . . . . .75.00
NUTCRACKER PRINCE — 8", #14571, 1995, Nutcracker Series, has mask 65.00

8" NURSES WITH BABIES, hard plastic. Both are bend knee walkers. Left in white is from 1960 – 61. Right in blue and white is from 1962 – 65.

Please read "What is a Price Guide?" for additional information.

O'BRIEN, MARGARET — 14½" compo., 1946–1948 . . . . .750.00
    17", 18", 19" compo., 1946–1948 . . . . .850.00–1,050.00
    21–24" compo., 1946–1948 . . . . .1,000.00–1,200.00
    14½" h.p., 1949–1951 . . . . .900.00
    17–18" h.p., 1949–1951 . . . . .975.00
    21–22" h.p., 1949–1951 . . . . .1,200.00 up
OKTOBERFEST — 8" (see Collectors Unlimited under Special Events/Exclusives) 125.00
OLD FASHIONED GIRL — 13" compo., 1945–1947 (Betty) . . . . .550.00 up
    20" compo. (Betty) 700.00
    20" h.p., 1948 only (Margaret) . . . . .800.00 up
    14" h.p., 1948 only (Margaret) 650.00
OLIVE OYL — 10", #20126, 1996, Timeless Legends 90.00
OLIVER TWIST — 16" cloth, 1934, Dickens character 650.00
    7" compo., 1935–1936 (Tiny Betty) 300.00
    8", #472, 1992 only, Storyland Series (Wendy Ann) 65.00
OLIVER TWISTAIL — Cloth/felt, 1930's 650.00
ONE, TWO, BUCKLE MY SHOE — 14", #24640, Nursery Rhymes (Louisa) 95.00
ONYX VELVET AND LACE GALA GOWN AND COAT — 10", h.p., #22170, 1997 . . . . .115.00
OPENING NIGHT — 10", #1126, 1989 only, Portrette, gold sheath and overshirt (Cissette) 85.00
OPHELIA — 12", 1992, Romance Collection (Nancy Drew) 115.00
    12", 1993 only (Lissy) 125.00
ORCHARD PRINCESS — 21" compo., 1939, 1946–1947, has extra makeup (Wendy Ann) . . . . .2,400.00 up
ORPHANT ANNIE — 14" plastic/vinyl, #1480, 1965–1966 only, Literature Series (Mary Ann) 350.00
    #1485, 1965 only, in window box with wardrobe . . . . .500.00 up

18" MARGARET O'BRIEN, 1946 – 48. All composition. All original with original box.

Close up of composition MARGARET O'BRIEN. Her face and clothing are extraordinary.

Please read "What is a Price Guide?" for additional information.

PAKISTAN — 8" h.p., #532, 1993 only 65.00
PAMELA — 12" h.p., 1962–1963 only, takes wigs, excellent condition, doll only (Lissy) ....350.00 up
    12" h.p. in case, 1962–1963 ....1,000.00 up
    12" h.p. in window box, 1962–1963 ....900.00 up
    12" plastic/vinyl, 1969–1971, doll only (Nancy Drew) 225.00
    12" plastic/vinyl in case, 1969 ....500.00 up
PAMELA PLAYS DRESS UP — 12" (see Horchow under Special Events/Exclusives) 225.00
PAN AMERICAN – (POLLERA) — 7" compo., 1936–1938 (Tiny Betty) 300.00
PANAMA — 8", #555, 1985–1987 ....65.00
PANDORA — 8", (see Dolls 'n Bearland under Special Events/Exclusives) 150.00
PARK AVENUE ALEX THE BELLHOP — 8", h.p., #31180, 1997, burgundy uniform 80.00
PARK AVENUE WENDY — 8", h.p., #31060, 1997, black and white ensemble 80.00
PARLOUR MAID — 8" h.p., #579, 1956 only (Wendy Ann) ....950.00 up
PAT-A-CAKE — 8", #12812, 1995, floral dress with white apron and chef's hat, Nursery Rhymes Series 55.00
PATCHITY PAM & PEPPER — 15" cloth, 1965–1966 ....175.00
PATTERSON, MARTHA JOHNSON — 1982–1984, 3rd set Presidents' Ladies/First Ladies Series (Martha) 125.00
PATTY — 18" plastic/vinyl, 1965 only 275.00
PATTY PIGTAILS — 14" h.p., 1949 only (Margaret) ....675.00 up
PAULETTE — 10", #1128, 1989–1990 only, Portrette, dressed in pink velvet (Cissette) 125.00
PEACHTREE LANE — 8" in blue and 14" SCARLETT in green/white stripes, #16551, limited to 2,500 .....250.00 set
PEARL (JUNE) — 10", #1150, 1992 only, Birthstone Collection, white/silver flapper doll 75.00
PEASANT — 7" compo., 1936–1937 (Tiny Betty) 275.00
    9" compo., 1938–1939 (Little Betty) 300.00
PEGGY BRIDE — 14–18" h.p., 1950–1951 (Margaret) 650.00
    21" h.p., 1950 ....800.00
PENNY — 34" cloth/vinyl, 1951 only ....500.00 up
    42", 1951 only 800.00
    7" compo., 1938–1940 (Tiny Betty) 250.00

8" PRINCESS ANN, 1957 only, #396.
All original. Bend knee walker.

22" PRINCESS FLAVIA, 1946. Character from the movie, *Prisoner of Zenda*. Composition.

PEPPERMINT TWIST — 8", #14591, 1995, pink skirt and jacket in 1950's style, Nostalgia Series 60.00

PERSIA — 7" compo., 1936–1938 (Tiny Betty) 300.00

PERU — 8", #556, 1986–1987 . . . . .85.00

    8" h.p., #531, 1993 only (Wendy Ann) 65.00

PERUVIAN BOY — 8" h.p., BK, #770, 1965–1966 (Wendy Ann) 425.00

    8" h.p., BKW, #770 . . . . .450.00

PETER PAN — 15" h.p., 1953–1954 (Margaret) . . . . .750.00 up

    8" h.p., #310, 1953–1954 (Wendy Ann) Quiz-kin . . . . .850.00 up

    8" h.p., #465, reintroduced 1991–1993, #140465 in 1994, Storyland Series (Wendy Ann) 75.00

    14" plastic/vinyl, #1410, 1969 only (Mary Ann) 250.00

        1969 only, complete set of 4 dolls –

        Peter, Michael (12" Jamie), Wendy (14" Mary Ann), Tinker Bell (10" Cissette) . . . . .1,100.00 up

PHILIPPINES — 8" straight leg, #554, 1986–1987 . . . . .95.00

    1987, #531, dressed in yellow gown 135.00

PICNIC DAY — 18" h.p., #2001C, 1953 only, Glamour Girl Series, leaves on pink or blue print dress

(Margaret) . . . . .1,400.00 up

PIERCE, JANE — 1982–1984, 3rd set Presidents' Ladies/First Ladies Series (Mary Ann) 125.00

PIERROT CLOWN — (see Clowns, 8" and 14")

PILGRIM — 7" compo., 1935–1938 (Tiny Betty) 275.00

    8" h.p., #100349, 1994, Americana Series 55.00

    8", #10349, 1995, Special Occasions Series 55.00

PINK CHAMPAGNE (ARLENE DAHL) — 18" h.p., red hair/pink lace/rhinestone bodice gown . . . . .5,500.00 up

PINKIE — 12" plastic/vinyl, 1975–1987, Portrait Children (Nancy Drew) 75.00

    8", 1997, #22120, chiffon gown, pink hat 70.00

PINKY — 16" cloth, 1940's 475.00

    23" compo./cloth baby, 1937–1939 . . . . .300.00

    13–19" vinyl baby, #3561, #5461, 1954 only, one-piece vinyl body and legs 75.00–125.00

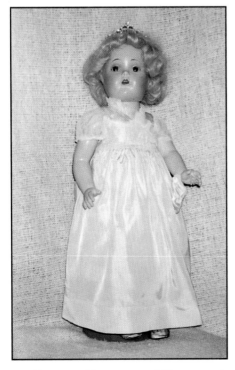

23" PRINCESS ELIZABETH. All composition, mohair wig. Yellow dress and bag. Tagged: "Lilli'bet." All rights reserved Madame Alexander N.Y.

PEGGY BRIDE, 1950–51. Hard plastic, "Margaret face." Mint condition.

PINOCCHIO — 8", #477, 1992–1993, Storyland Series (Wendy Ann) #140477, 1994 . . . . .65.00
PIP — All cloth, early 1930's, Dickens character 800.00
    7" compo., 1935–1936 (Tiny Betty) 300.00
PIPPI LONGSTOCKING — 18", #16003, 1996, Rag Dolls (cloth doll) 50.00
PITTY PAT — 16" cloth, 1950's 475.00
PITTY PAT CLOWN — 1950's 450.00
PLACE IN THE SUN, A — 10", #24624, lavender ball gown 110.00
PLAYMATES — 29" cloth, 1940's . . . . .450.00 up
POCAHONTAS — 8" h.p., BK, #721, 1967–1970, Americana & Storyland Series, has baby (Wendy Ann) 425.00
    8" h.p., #318, 1991–1992, Americana Series (Wendy Ann) 65.00
    8" h.p., #100350, 1994—1995, Americana & Favorite Book Series (Wendy Ann) 55.00
    14", #24613, 1995, first dark skin doll this size, Favorite Books Series (Louisa) 90.00
POLISH (POLAND) — 7" compo., 1935–1936 (Tiny Betty) 275.00
    8" h.p., BKW, #780, 1964–1965 (Wendy Ann) 125.00
    8" BKW, #780, 1965 only (Maggie Mixup) 150.00
    8" h.p., BK, #780, 1965–1972 . . . . .100.00
    8" h.p., straight leg, #0780, #580, 1973–1975, marked "ALEX." .75.00
    8" straight leg, #580, 1976–1988 (1985–1987 white face), marked "Alexander" 65.00
    8", #523, reintroduced 1992–1993 (Maggie Mixup) 1994, #110523 .60.00
POLK, SARAH — 1979–1981, 2nd set Presidents' Ladies/First Ladies Series (Martha) 135.00
POLLERA (PAN AMERICAN) — 7" compo., 1936–1938 (Tiny Betty) 275.00
POLLY — 17" plastic/vinyl, 1965 only, dressed in ballgown 375.00
    Dressed in street dress 275.00
    Dressed as ballerina 300.00
    Dressed as bride 300.00
    1965 only, came in trunk with wardrobe . . . . .750.00 up
POLLY FLINDERS — 8", #443, 1988–1989, Storybook Series (Maggie) 85.00
POLLY PIGTAILS — 14½" h.p., 1949–1951 (Maggie) 500.00
    17–17½", 1949–1951 . . . . .625.00
    8" (see M.A.D.C. under Special Events/Exclusives) 150.00
POLLY PUT KETTLE ON — 7" compo., 1937–1939 (Tiny Betty) 275.00
POLLYANA — 16" rigid vinyl, 1960–1961, marked "1958" (Marybel) 425.00
    16", dressed in formal 475.00
    22", 1960–1961 . . . . .500.00
    14", #1588, 1987–1988, Classic Series (Mary Ann) 90.00
    14", reintroduced 1994 only, #24159 . . . . .100.00
    8", #474, 1992–1993 only, Storyland Series (Maggie Mixup) 65.00
POODLES — 14–17", early 1950's, standing or sitting, named **IVY, PIERRE,** and **FIFI** . . . . . . .350.00 up
POOR CINDERELLA — (see Cinderella)
POPEYE — 8", #10428, 1996, Timeless Legends 85.00
POPEYE, OLIVE OYL, AND SWEET PEA — #20127, 1996 . . . . .175.00 set
POPPY — 9" early vinyl, 1953 only, orange organdy dress & bonnet 95.00
PORTRAIT ELISE — 17" plastic/vinyl, 1972–1973 . . . . .200.00
PORTUGAL — 8" h.p., BK, #785, 1968–1972 (Wendy Ann) 100.00
    8" straight leg, #0785, #585, 1973–1975, marked "Alex." 75.00
    8" straight leg, #585, #537, 1976–1987, marked "Alexander" 65.00
    8", #537, 1986, white face 55.00
    8" h.p., #535, 1993, #110535, 1994 . . . . .50.00
POSEY PET — 15" cloth, 1940's, plush rabbit or other animals, must be clean 450.00
PRECIOUS — 12" compo./cloth baby, 1937–1940 . . . . .250.00
    12" all h.p. toddler, 1948–1951 . . . . .350.00
PREMIER DOLLS — 8", (see M.A.D.C. under Special Events/Exclusives)
PRESIDENTS' LADIES/FIRST LADIES —
    1st set, 1976–1978 .150.00–175.00 singles . . . . . 1,000.00 set
    2nd set, 1979–1981 . . . . .125.00 singles . . . . 800.00 set

PRESIDENTS' LADIES/FIRST LADIES, CONTINUED . . .

3rd set, 1982–1984	125.00 singles	800.00 set
4th set, 1985–1987	125.00 singles	700.00 set
5th set, 1988	125.00 singles	700.00 set
6th set, 1989–1990	125.00 singles	700.00 set

PRINCE CHARLES — 8" h.p., #397, 1957 only (Wendy Ann) .....750.00 up
PRINCE CHARMING — 16–17" compo., 1947 (Margaret) 750.00
    14–15" h.p., 1948–1950 (Margaret) 700.00
    17–18" h.p., 1948–1950 (Margaret) 850.00
    21" h.p., 1949–1951 (Margaret) 1,000.00
    12", 1990–1991, Romance Collection (Nancy Drew) 85.00
    8", #479, 1993, Storybook Series, royal blue/gold outfit 75.00
    8", #14541, 1995, Brothers Grimm Series, braid trimmed jacket with brocade vest 65.00
PRINCE PHILLIP — 17–18" h.p., 1953 only, Beaux Arts Series (Margaret) 850.00
    21", 1953 only 975.00
PRINCESS — 12", 1990–1991 only, Romance Collection (Nancy Drew) 85.00
    14", #1537, 1990 - Mary Ann; 1991 - Jennifer, Classic Series 100.00
    20" h.p., 1955 only, Child's Dream Comes True Series (Cissy) .....985.00 up
PRINCESS ALEXANDRIA — 24" cloth/compo., 1937 only .....275.00 up
PRINCESS ANN — 8" h.p., #396, 1957 only (Wendy Ann) .....800.00 up
PRINCESS BUDIR AL-BUDOR — 8", #483, 1993–1994 only, Storybook Series 65.00
PRINCESS DOLL — 13–15" compo., 1940–1942 (Princess Elizabeth) .....550.00 up
    24" compo., 1940–1942 (Princess Elizabeth) .....850.00 up
PRINCESS ELIZABETH — 7" compo., 1937–1939 (Tiny Betty) 350.00
    8", 1937, with Dionne head (**rare**) 400.00
    9–11" compo., 1937–1941 (Little Betty) 375.00–425.00
    13" compo., 1937–1941, with closed mouth (Betty) .....625.00 up
    14" compo., 1937–1941 .....600.00 up

17" POLLY, 1965, #1751. Made of soft vinyl. Mauve pleated tulle formal.

16" POLLYANNA, 1960, #1530. Plastic/vinyl "Marybel." Mint and all original.

PRINCESS ELIZABETH, CONTINUED . . .

    15" compo., open mouth . . . . .600.00 up

    18–19" compo., 1937–1941, open mouth 700.00

    24" compo., 1938–1939, open mouth . . . . .850.00 up

    28" compo., 1938–1939, open mouth . . . . .1,000.00 up

PRINCESS FLAVIA (ALSO VICTORIA) — 21" compo., 1939, 1946–1947 (Wendy Ann) . . . . .2,000.00 up

PRINCESS MARGARET ROSE — 15–18" compo., 1937–1938 (Princess Elizabeth) .800.00 up

    21" compo., 1938 . . . . .975.00

    14–18" h.p., 1949–1953 (Margaret) 700.00–975.00

    18" h.p., #2020B, 1953 only, Beaux Arts Series, pink taffeta gown with red ribbon, tiara (Margaret) . .1,700.00

PRINCESS ROSETTA — 21" compo., 1939, 1946–1947 (Wendy Ann) 2,300.00

PRISTINE ANGEL — 10", #10604, 100th Anniversary, second in series, white/gold 95.00

PRISCILLA — 18" cloth, mid 1930's 625.00

    7" compo., 1935–1938 (Tiny Betty) 275.00

    8" h.p., BK, #729, 1965–1970, Americana & Storybook Series (Wendy Ann) 350.00

PRISSY — 8", #630, 1990 only, Scarlett Series (Wendy Ann) 95.00

    8", #637, reintroduced 1992–1993 . . . . .75.00

    8", #16650, 1995, Scarlett Series, floral gown 55.00

PROM QUEEN (MEMORIES) — 8" (see M.A.D.C. under Special Events/Exclusives) 250.00

PUDDIN' — 14–21" cloth/vinyl, 1966–1975 . . . . .85.00

    14–18", 1987 . . . . .75.00–95.00

    14–21", 1990–1993 . . . . .75.00–100.00

    14" only, 1994–1995 . . . . .85.00

    21", 1995 . . . . .100.00

PUMPKIN — 22" cloth/vinyl, 1967–1976 . . . . .125.00

    22", 1976 only, with rooted hair 150.00

PUPPET, HAND (ALSO SEE MARIONETTES) — Compo. head, cloth hand mitt body, by Tony Sarg, ca. 1936 . . .225.00 up

PUSS 'N BOOTS — 8", #14552, Fairy Tales Series 65.00

PUSSY CAT — Cloth/vinyl.

    WHITE DOLLS:

        14", 1965–1985 (20 year production) 75.00

        14", 1987–1995 . . . . .75.00

        14", 1966, 1968, in trunk/trousseau . . . . .250.00 up

        18", 1989–1995 . . . . .125.00

        20", 1965–1984, 1987–1988 (20+ year production) 100.00

        24", 1965–1985 (20 year production) 125.00

    BLACK DOLLS:

        14", 1970–1976 . . . . .100.00

        14", 1984–1995 (12 year production) 75.00

        20", 1976–1983 . . . . .125.00

PUSSY CAT, LIVELY — 14", 20", 24", 1966–1969 only, knob makes head & limbs move 100.00–175.00

Please read "What is a Price Guide?" for additional information.

QUEEN — 18" h.p., #2025, 1953 only, Beaux Arts Series, white gown, long velvet cape trimmed with fur
(Margaret) 1,500.00
18" h.p., 1953 only, Glamour Girl Series, same gown/tiara as above but no cape (Margaret) 850.00
18" h.p., 1954 only, Me & My Shadow Series, white gown, short Orlon cape (Margaret) 975.00
8" h.p., 1954, #0030C, #597, Me & My Shadow Series, Orlon cape attached to purple robe
(Wendy Ann) ....1,200.00 up
8", #499, 1955 only, scarlet velvet robe 850.00
10" h.p., #971, #879, #842, #763, 1957–1958, 1960–1961, gold gown with blue ribbon 375.00
#742, #765, 1959, 1963, white gown with blue ribbon 350.00
#1186, #1187, 1972–1973, white gown with red ribbon 350.00
1959, in trunk with wardrobe, must be mint ....900.00 up
14", #1536, 1990 only, Classic Series (Louisa, Jennifer) 90.00
20" h.p./vinyl arms, 1955, Dreams Come True Series, white brocade gown (Cissy) 1,200.00
1957, Fashion Parade Series, white gown 900.00
1958, 1961–1963 (1958 - Dolls To Remember Series), gold gown 775.00

8" QUEEN ELIZABETH, 1954. From the Me and My Shadow Series. Straight leg walker. Notice the purple robe that was only made in 1954.

8" QUIZKIN, 1953 only. Straight leg non-walker.

QUEEN, CONTINUED . . .

18", 1963 only, white gown with red ribbon (Elise) 700.00

    With vinyl head (Marybel) 850.00

18" vinyl, same as 1965 (21" with rooted hair, 1966 only), gold brocade gown, rare doll (Elise) 975.00

#2150, 21" h.p./vinyl arms, 1965, white brocade gown (Jacqueline) 750.00

    1968, gold gown 750.00

QUEEN ALEXANDRINE — 21" compo., 1939–1941 (Wendy Ann) 1,975.00

QUEEN CHARLOTTE — 10", (see M.A.D.C. under Special Events/Exclusives) 350.00

QUEEN ELIZABETH I — 10", (see My Doll House under Special Events/Exclusives) 150.00

QUEEN ELIZABETH II — 8", 1992 only (mid-year issue), commemorating reign's 40th anniversary 150.00

QUEEN ESTHER — 8", #14584, 1995 only, Bible Series 100.00

QUEEN OF HEARTS — 8" straight leg, #424, 1987–1990, Storybook Series (Wendy Ann) 75.00

    8", #14511, 1995, Alice In Wonderland Series 72.00

10", (see Disney under Special Events/Exclusives) 400.00

QUEEN ISABELLA — 8" h.p., #329, 1992 only, Americana Series 125.00

QUINTUPLETS (FISCHER QUINTS) — 7", h.p. & vinyl 1964 (Genius) . . . . .550.00 set

QUIZ-KINS — 8" h.p., 1953, bald head, in romper only (Wendy Ann) . . . . .475.00 up

1953 Peter Pan, caracul wig 800.00

1953–1954, as groom . . . . .575.00 up

1953–1954, as bride . . . . .625.00 up

1953–1954, girl with wig, ...650.00 up

1953, girl without wig, in romper suit 600.00

8" QUIZKIN BRIDE and GROOM, 1953. Straight leg non-walker. Both have Yes and No buttons on their back.

Please read "What is a Price Guide?" for additional information.

RACHEL/RACHAEL — 8", 1989 (see Belks & Leggett under Special Events/Exclusives) 75.00
RANDOLPH, MARTHA — 1976–1978, 1st set Presidents' Ladies/First Ladies Series (Louisa) 150.00
RAPUNZEL — 10", #M31, 1989–1992 only, Portrette, gold velvet (Cissette) 125.00
    14", #1539, 1993–1994, Doll Classics, limited to 3,000, comes with 8" Mother Gothel 250.00
    14", #87005, 1996, purple gown (Louisa) 125.00
    8", #14542, 1995, Brothers Grimm Series, pink gown with gold scallops, #1398, 1997 . . . . .75.00
REALLY UGLY STEPSISTER — 8", h.p., #13450, 1997, Cinderella Series 85.00
REBECCA — 14–17", 21" compo., 1940–1941 (Wendy Ann) . . . . .600.00–1,000.00 up
    14" h.p., 1948–1949 (Margaret) . . . . .850.00 up
    14" plastic/vinyl, #1485, 1968–1969, Classic Series, two-tiered skirt in pink (Mary Ann) 175.00
        #1485, #1515, #1585, 1970–1985, one-piece skirt, pink pindot or check dress 85.00
        #1586, 1986–1987, blue dress with striped pinafore 85.00
    8", #14647, 1996 . . . . .57.00
RECORD ALBUM — "Madame Alexander Collector's Album," 1978, Children's stories told by Madame.
    Cover is like Alexander box 35.00
RED BOY — 8" h.p., BK, #740, 1972 (Wendy Ann) 125.00
    #0740, 1973–1975, marked "Alex." 75.00
    #440, 1976–1988 (1985–1987 white face), marked "Alexander" 65.00
RED CROSS NURSE — 18", #16002, Rag Doll Series 50.00
RED RIDING HOOD — 7" compo., 1936–1942 (Tiny Betty) 275.00
    9" compo., 1939–1940 (Little Betty) 300.00
    8" h.p., SLW, #608, 1955, cape sewn under arms (Wendy Ann) 550.00
    8" h.p., BKW, #382, 1962–1965, Storybook Series (Wendy Ann) 275.00
    8" h.p., BK, #782, 1965–1972 . . . . .125.00
    8" h.p., straight leg, #0782, #482, 1973–1975, marked "Alex." 75.00
    8" h.p., straight leg, #482, 1976–1986 (1985–1987 white face), marked "Alexander" 65.00

RENOIR GIRL, 1986, #1572. Made one year only. Pink pleated nylon dress.

8" RED RIDING HOOD, 1955, #471. Straight leg walker. Mint and all original.

RED RIDING HOOD, CONTINUED . . .

8", #485, #463, 1987–1991 (Maggie), 1992–1993 (Wendy Ann), #140463–1994	.65.00
14", #24617, 1995, patchwork dress with red cape (Mary Ann)	.100.00
14", #87004, plaid dress with red cape (Mary Ann)	.65.00

RED SHOES — 8", #14533, 1995, ballerina with same head as **SPAIN** 60.00
RED QUEEN — 8", h.p., 1997, #13010, red and gold gown 120.00
RED QUEEN AND WHITE KING SET — 8" pair, #13030, 1997 ....210.00
RENOIR — 21" compo., 1945–1946, extra makeup, must be excellent (Wendy Ann) 2,000.00

14" h.p., 1950 only (Margaret)	.875.00 up
21" h.p./vinyl arms, 1961 only (Cissy)	.825.00 up
18" h.p./vinyl arms, vinyl head, 1963 only (Elise)	.575.00 up
#2154, 21" h.p./vinyl arms, 1965, pink gown (Jacqueline)	.700.00
#2062, 1966, blue gown with black trim (Coco)	.2,200.00
#2175, 1967, navy blue gown, red hat	.650.00
#2194, #2184, 1969–1970, blue gown, full lace overdress	.650.00
#2163, 1971, all yellow gown	.650.00
#2190, 1972, pink gown with black jacket & trim	.600.00
#2190, 1973, yellow gold gown, black ribbon	.550.00
10" h.p., #1175, 1968, all navy with red hat (Cissette)	.450.00
#1175, 1969, pale blue gown, short jacket, stripe or dotted skirt	.475.00
#1180, 1970, all aqua satin	.425.00

RENOIR CHILD — 12" plastic/vinyl, #1274, 1967 only, Portrait Children Series (Nancy Drew) 150.00
14", #1474, 1968 only (Mary Ann) 175.00

RENOIR GIRL — 14" plastic/vinyl, #1469, #1475, 1967–1968, Portrait Children Series, white dress with red ribbon trim, (Mary Ann) 175.00
    #1477, 1969–1971, pink dress, white pinafore 90.00
    #1477, #1478, #1578, 1972–1986 (14 year production), pink multi-tiered lace gown 85.00
    #1572, 1986 only, pink pleated nylon dress 75.00
RENOIR GIRL WITH WATERING CAN — #1577, 1985–1987, Classic & Fine Arts Series 85.00
    8", h.p., #22150, 1997, navy taffeta dress 70.00
RENOIR GIRL WITH HOOP — #1574, 1986–1987, Classic & Fine Arts Series 95.00
RENOIR MOTHER — 21" h.p./vinyl arms, 1967 only, navy blue, red hat (Jacqueline) ....900.00 up
RHETT — 12", #1380, 1981–1985, Portrait Children Series, black jacket/grey pants (Nancy Drew) 85.00
    8", #401, 1989 only, Jubilee II (Wendy Ann) 100.00
    8", #632, #642, 1991–1992 only, Scarlett Series, all white/blue vest 85.00
    8", #642, 1993, #160642, 1994, tan pants/vest/tie with white jacket 80.00
    10", h.p., #15050, 1997, *Gone with the Wind* Series 95.00
RIDING HABIT — 8", 1990 only, Americana Series (Wendy Ann) 75.00
    #571, 1956 ....475.00
    #373G, 1957 ....475.00
    #541, 1958 ....550.00
    #355, 1962 ....350.00
    #623, 1965 ....325.00
RILEY'S LITTLE ANNIE — 14" plastic/vinyl, #1481, 1967 only, Literature Series (Mary Ann) 225.00
RING AROUND THE ROSEY — 8", #12813, Nursery Rhymes Series 60.00
RINGBEARER — 14" h.p., 1951 only, must be near mint (Lovey Dove) ....550.00 up
RINGMASTER — 8" (see Collectors United under Special Events/Exclusives) 125.00
RIVERBOAT QUEEN (LENA) — (see M.A.D.C. under Special Events/Exclusives) 300.00
ROBIN HOOD — 8", #446, 1988–1990, Storybook Series (Wendy Ann) 60.00
ROCK AND ROLL GROUP — #22110, 1997, four 8" dolls, mod costumes 300.00

**14" RENOIR GIRL, with watering can,
1985 – 87, #1577. Plastic/vinyl.**

RODEO — 8" h.p., #483, 1955 only (Wendy Ann) . . . . .900.00 up
RODEO ROSIE — 14", #87012, 1996, red checked western costume 125.00
ROGERS, GINGER — 14–21" compo., 1940–1945 (Wendy Ann) . . . . .2,500.00 up
ROLLER BLADES — 8", "Throughly Modern Wendy" (see Disney under Special Events/Exclusives) 100.00
ROLLER SKATING — 8" h.p., SL, SLW, BK, #556, 1953–1956 (Wendy Ann) . . . . .500.00 up
ROMANCE — 21" compo., 1945–1946, extra makeup, must be mint (Wendy Ann) 2,100.00
ROMEO — 18" compo., 1949 (Wendy Ann) . . . . .1,400.00 up
    8" h.p., #474, 1955 only (Wendy Ann) . . . . .950.00 up
    12" plastic/vinyl, #1370, 1978–1987, Portrait Children Series (Nancy Drew) 75.00
    12", reintroduced 1991–1992 only, Romance Collection (Nancy Drew) 80.00
    8", 1994, mid-year introduction (see M.A.D.C. under Special Events/Exclusives) 125.00
ROOSEVELT, EDITH — 1988, 5th set Presidents' Ladies/First Ladies Series (Louisa) 125.00
ROOSEVELT, ELEANOR — 14", 1989–1990, 6th set Presidents' Ladies/First Ladies Series (Louisa) 135.00
ROSAMUND BRIDESMAID — 15" h.p., 1951 only (Margaret, Maggie) . . . . .500.00 up
    17–18" h.p., 1951 only (Margaret, Maggie) . . . . .600.00 up
ROSE — 9" early vinyl toddler, 1953 only, pink organdy dress & bonnet 125.00
ROSEBUD — 16–19" cloth/vinyl, 1952–1953 . . . . .125.00
    13", 1953 only 150.00
    23–25", 1953 only 175.00
ROSEBUD (PUDDIN') — 14"–20", 1986 only, white 50.00
    14", black 75.00
ROSE FAIRY — 8" h.p., #622, 1956 only (Wendy Ann) . . . . .1,400.00 up
ROSETTE — 10", #1115, 1987–1989, Portrette, pink/rose gown (Cissette) 100.00
ROSEY POSEY — 14" cloth/vinyl, 1976 only 65.00
    21" cloth/vinyl, 1976 only 100.00
ROSS, BETSY — 8" h.p., Americana Series, 1967–1972 (Wendy Ann)
    Bend knees, #731 . . . . .100.00
    Straight legs, #0731, #431, 1973–1975, Storybook Series, marked "Alex" 75.00
    Straight legs, #431, 1976–1987 (1985–1987 white face) 65.00
    8", #312, reintroduced 1991–1992 only, Americana Series 60.00
    #312, 1976 Bicentennial gown (star print) 125.00
ROSY — 14", #1562, 1988–1990, Classic Series, all pink dress with cream lace trim (Mary Ann) 85.00
ROUND UP COWGIRL — 8" (see Disney under Special Events/Exclusives) 125.00
ROYAL EVENING — 18" h.p., 1953 only, cream/royal blue gown (Margaret) . . . . .2,400.00 up
ROYAL WEDDING — 21" compo., 1939 only, full circles trimmed in lace on lower skirt (Wendy Ann) 3,250.00
ROXANNE — 8" h.p., #140504, 1994 only, Storyland Series 65.00
ROZY — 12" plastic/vinyl, #1130, 1969 only (Janie) 375.00
RUBY (JULY) — 10", #1151, 1992 only, Birthstone Collection, all red/gold (Cissette) 75.00
RUFFLES CLOWN — 21", 1954 only 425.00
RUMANIA — 8" h.p., BK, #786, 1968–1972 (Wendy Ann) 100.00
    8" straight leg, #0786, #586, 1973–1975, marked "Alex." 75.00
    8" straight leg, #586, #538, 1976–1987, marked "Alexander" .65.00
    8", #538, 1986–1987 (1986 white face) 55.00
RUMBERA/RUMBERO — 7" compo., 1938–1943 (Tiny Betty) .350.00 each
    9" compo., 1939–1941 (Little Betty) . . . . .375.00 each
RUMPELSTILTSKIN & MILLER'S DAUGHTER — 8" & 14", #1569, 1992 only, limited to 3,000 sets . . . . .300.00 set
RUSSIA — 8" h.p., BK, #774, 1968–1972 (Wendy Ann) 100.00
    8" straight leg, #0774, 1973–1975, marked "Alex." 75.00
    8" straight leg, #574, #548, 1976–1988 (1985–1987 white face), marked "Alexander" 60.00
    8", #548, 1985–1987, white face 60.00
    8", #581, 1991–1992 only 55.00
    8", #110540, 1994 only, long blue gown with gold trim 55.00
RUSSIAN — 7" compo., 1935–1938 (Tiny Betty) 250.00
    9" compo., 1938–1942 (Little Betty) 300.00
RUSTY — 20" cloth/vinyl, 1967–1968 only 300.00

···◗ S ◖···

Please read "What is a Price Guide?" for additional information.

SAILOR — 14" compo., 1942–1945 (Wendy Ann) 750.00
    17" compo., 1943–1944 . . . . .875.00
    8" boy, 1990 (see U.F.D.C. under Special Events/Exclusives) 750.00
    8" boy, 1991 (see FAO Schwarz under Special Events/Exclusives) 100.00
    COLUMBIAN SAILOR— (see U.F.D.C. under Special Events/Exclusives) 275.00
SAILORETTE — 10" h.p., #1119, 1988 only, Portrette Series, red/white/blue outfit (Cissette) 75.00
SALLY BRIDE — 14" compo., 1938–1939 (Wendy Ann) . . . . .450.00 up
    18–21" compo., 1938–1939 . . . . .500.00–575.00
SALOME — 14", #1412, 1984–1986, Opera Series (Mary Ann) .90.00
SAMANTHA — 14" 1989 (see FAO Schwarz under Special Events/Exclusives) 150.00
    14", #1561, 1991–1992 only, Classic Series, gold ruffled gown (Mary Ann) 175.00
    10", h.p., #15300, from the *Bewitched* TV series 105.00
SAMSON — 8", #14582, 1995 only, Bible Series 100.00
SANDY MCHARE — Cloth/felt, 1930's 675.00
SANTA CLAUS — 14", #24608, 1995, Christmas Series 90.00
SANTA AND MRS. CLAUS — 8", mid-year issue (see Madame Alexander Doll Co. under
  Special Events/Exclusives) . . . . .75.00 each
SAPPHIRE (SEPTEMBER) — 10", 1992 only, Birthstone Collection 85.00
SARDINIA — 8", #509, 1989–1991 only (Wendy Ann) 60.00
SARGENT — 14", #1576, 1984–1985, Fine Arts Series, dressed in lavender (Mary Ann) 85.00
SARGENT'S GIRL — 14", #1579, 1986 only, Fine Arts Series, dressed in pink (Mary Ann) 85.00
SCARECROW — 8", #430, 1993, #140430, 1994–1996, Storybook Series and Wizard of Oz Series, #13230, 1997 . .60.00
SCARLETT O'HARA — (Before movie, 1937–1938)
    7" compo., 1937–1942 (Tiny Betty) 450.00
    9" compo., 1938–1941 (Little Betty) 500.00
    11", 1937–1942 (Wendy Ann) 650.00
    14–15" compo., 1941–1943 (Wendy Ann) 800.00
    18" compo., 1939–1946 (Wendy Ann) 1,250.00

8" OLYMPIA. Made for 1996 C.U. Gathering in honor of the Olympics held in Atlanta.

8" GRETA from C.U. Gathering's Jacksonville event in 1996 honoring Greta Schrader of the Alexander Doll Co.

SCARLETT O'HARA, CONTINUED . . .

21" compo., 1945, 1947 (Wendy Ann) 1,600.00

14–16" h.p., 1950s (Margaret) 1,600.00

14–16" h.p., 1950s (Maggie) 1,650.00

20" h.p., 1950s (Margaret) . . . . .1,800.00 up

21", 1955, blue taffeta gown w/black looped braid trim, short jacket (Cissy) . . . . .1,300.00 up

   1958, jointed arms, green velvet jacket and bonnet trimmed in light green net. Rare . . . . .2,000.00 up

   1961–1962, straight arms, white organdy, green ribbon inserted into tiers of lace on skirt,

      white picture hat, *rare* . . . . .2,000.00 up

18" h.p./vinyl arms, 1963 only, pale blue organdy w/rosebuds, straw hat (Elise) . . . . .850.00 up

12" h.p., 1963 only, green taffeta gown and bonnet (Lissy) 1,400.00

7½–8", 1953–1954, white gown w/red rosebuds, white lace hat (Wendy Ann) . . . . .1,300.00 up

7½–8" h.p., #485, 1955, two layer gown, white/yellow/green trim (Wendy Ann) . . . . .1,400.00 up

8" h.p., BKW, 1956, pink, blue, or yellow floral gown . . . . .1,250.00 up

8" h.p., BKW, #431, 1957, white, lace and ribbon trim (dress must be mint) . . . . .1,400.00 up

8" h.p., BK, #760, 1963 . . . . .650.00 up

8", BK, 1965, in white or cream gown (Wendy Ann) . . . . .700.00 up

8", BK, 1971 only, bright pink floral print 650.00

8", BK, #725, 1966–1972, Americana & Storybook Series, floral gown 375.00

8", #0725, #425, 1973–1991 (18 year production), white gown (Wendy Ann) 85.00

   Straight leg, #425, #426, 1976–1986 (1985–1986 white face), marked "Alexander" 75.00

      #426, 1987 white face, blue dot gown 225.00

   Straight leg, #426, 1988–1989, floral gown 85.00

   1986 (see M.A.D.C. under Special Events/Exclusives) 225.00

   1989, #400, Jubilee II, green velvet/gold trim 150.00

   Straight leg, #626, 1990 only, tiny floral print 85.00

   #631, 1991 only, 3-tier white gown, curly hair 85.00

   #627, 1992 only, rose floral print, oversized bonnet 85.00

   #641, 1993, white gown with green stripes and trim 75.00

   #643, 1993, #160643, 1994 (Honeymoon In New Orleans), trunk with wardrobe 275.00

   #160644, 1994 only, **SCARLETT BRIDE** 85.00

9" and 14" SWEET TEARS. All original with poodle from layette set. Soft vinyl.

***SCARLETT O'HARA*, CONTINUED . . .**

#160647, 1994 only, **SCARLETT PICNIC**, green/red floral on white, large ruffle at hem 95.00
#16648, 1995–1996, white four-tiered organdy gown with red trim 75.00
#16652, 1995 only, floral print picnic outfit with organdy overskirt 85.00
#16553, green drapery gown, 100th Anniversary 100.00
#16653, 1996, Ashley's Farewell, maroon taffeta skirt 75.00
#17025, 1996, Tomorrow is Another Day, floral gown 65.00
#86004, 1996, Ashley's Birthday, red velvet gown 100.00
#15030, 1997, Shadow, rose picnic dress 80.00
8" h.p., 1990, M.A.D.C. Symposium (see M.A.D.C. Special Events/Exclusives) 175.00
8", 1993, mid-year issue (see Madame Alexander Doll Co. under Special Events/Exclusives) 100.00
21" h.p./vinyl arms, #2153, 1963–1964 (became "Godey" in 1965 with blonde hair) . . . . .1,500.00 up
21" h.p./vinyl arms, 1965, #2152, green satin gown (Jacqueline) . . . . .1,800.00 up
#2061, 1966, all white gown, red sash & roses (also with plain wide lace hem; also inverted "V"
scalloped lace hem – allow more for this gown) (Coco) 2,700.00
#2174, 1967, green satin gown with black trim 675.00
#2180, 1968, floral print gown with wide white hem . . . . .1,000.00 up
#2190, 1969, red gown with white lace 650.00
#2180, 1970, green satin, white trim on jacket 650.00
#2292, 2295, 2296, 1975–1977, all green satin, white lace at cuffs 450.00
#2110, 1978, silk floral gown, green parasol, white lace 500.00
#2240, 1979–1985, green velvet 350.00
#2255, 1986 only, floral gown, green parasol, white lace 350.00
#2247, 1987–1988, layered all over white gown 325.00
#2253, 1989, doll has full bangs, all red gown (Birthday Party gown) 400.00
#2258, 1990–1993 only, Scarlett Bride, Scarlett Series 375.00
#2259, 1991–1992 only, green on white, three ruffles around skirt .350.00
21" #162276, 1994, (Jacqueline) tight green gown, three layered bustle 300.00
#009, porcelain, 1991 only, green velvet, gold trim 600.00
#50001, Scarlett Picnic (Jacqueline), floral gown 310.00
#15020, rose picnic dress, carries garden basket 375.00
10" h.p., #1174, 1968 only, lace in bonnet, green satin gown with black braid trim (Cissette) 450.00
#1174, 1969, green satin gown with white & gold braid 425.00
#1181, #1180, 1970–1973, green satin gown with gold braid trim .400.00
10" h.p., #1100, 1989 only, Jubilee II, burgundy and white 150.00
#1102, 1990–1991 only, Scarlett Series, floral print gown 150.00
10", #1105, 1992 only, Scarlett at Ball, all in black 125.00
10", 1993, #161105, 1994, green velvet drapes/gold trim 125.00
10", 1994–1995, Scarlett in red dress with red boa 125.00
10", #16107, 1995 only, white sheath with dark blue jacket 100.00
10", #16654, 1996, mourning dress 110.00
10", #16656, 1996, Scarlett and Rhett, limited set 210.00
10", #15000, 1997, Hoop-Petti outfit 105.00
10", #15040, 1997, mourning outfit 115.00
12", 1981–1985, green gown with braid trim (Nancy Drew) 125.00
14" plastic/vinyl, #1495, 1968 only, floral gown (Mary Ann) 450.00
#1490, #7590, 1969–1986 (18 year production), white gown, tagged "Gone With The Wind"
(Mary Ann) 100.00
#1590, #1591, 1987–1989, blue or green floral print on beige 140.00
#1590, 1990, Scarlett Series, tiny floral print gown 150.00
#1595, 1991–1992 only, Scarlett Series, white ruffles, green ribbon (Louisa, Jennifer) 140.00
#16551, 1995 (see **PEACHTREE LANE**)
#1500, 14", 1986 only, Jubilee #1, all green velvet (Mary Ann) 200.00
#1300, 14", 1989 only, Jubilee #2, green floral print gown (Mary Ann) 150.00
SCARLETT, MISS — 14" (see Belks & Leggett under Special Events/Exclusives) 150.00

Scarlett O'Hara, continued . . .

School Girl — 7" compo., 1936–1943 (Tiny Betty) 275.00

Scotch — 7" compo., 1936–1939 (Tiny Betty) 275.00

    9" compo., 1939–1940 (Little Betty) 350.00

    10" h.p., 1962–1963 (Cissette) . . . . .900.00 up

Scots Lass — 8" h.p., BKW, #396, 1963 only (Maggie Mixup, Wendy Ann) . . . . .300.00 up

Scottish (Scotland) — 8" h.p., BKW, #796, 1964–1965 (Wendy Ann) 150.00

    8" h.p., BK, #796, 1965–1972 (Wendy Ann) 125.00

    8" straight leg, #0796-596, 1973–1975, marked "ALEX." 85.00

    8" straight leg, #596, #529, 1976–1993 (1985–1987 white face), marked "Alexander" 70.00

    8" redressed, Scot outfit with English guard hat, 1994 . . . . .65.00

Scout — 8", #367, 1991–1992 only, Americana Series 65.00

Scrooge — 14", #18401, 1996, Dickens (Mary Ann) 125.00

Sears Roebuck — (see Special Events/Exclusives)

Secret Garden, My — 8" (see FAO Schwarz under Special Events/Exclusives) 350.00

    14", #24616, 1995, has trunk and wardrobe (Louisa) 225.00

September — 14", #1527, 1989 only, Classic Series (Mary Ann) 85.00

    10", #1152, 1992, Portrette, royal blue/gold flapper 100.00

Seven Dwarfs — Compo., 1937 only, must be mint . . . . .475.00 each

Shadow of Madame — (see Doll & Teddy Bear Expo under Special Events/Exclusives) 275.00

Shadow Stepmother — 8", #14638, 1996 . . . . .70.00

Shaharazad — 10", #1144, 1992–1993 only, Portrette (Cissette) 85.00

She Sells Seashells — 8", #14629, 1996, Nursery Rhyme (Maggie) 70.00

Shea Elf — 8" (see Collectors United under Special Events/Exclusives) 200.00

Shepherd and Drummer Boy Set — 8", #19490, 1997, Nativity set 160.00

Shirley's Doll House — (see Special Events/Exclusives)

Shoemaker's Elf Boy — 8", #14637, 1996 . . . . .65.00

Shoemaker's Elf Girl — 8", #14636, 1996 . . . . .65.00

Sicily — 8", #513, 1989–1990 (Wendy Ann) 75.00

Simone — 21" h.p./vinyl arms, 1968 only, in trunk (Jacqueline) . . . . .2,150.00 up

Sir Lapin Hare — Cloth/felt, 1930's 700.00

Sister Brenda — (see FAO Schwarz under Special Events/Exclusives) . . . . .175.00 set

Sitting Pretty — 18" foam body, 1965 only, *rare* . . . . .400.00 up

Skater's Waltz — 15"–18", 1955–1956 (Cissy) 650.00

Skating Doll — 16", 1947–1950, (untagged "Sonja Henie" after contract expired) 700.00

Sleeping Beauty — 7–9" compo., 1941–1944 (Tiny Betty & Little Betty) 350.00–400.00

    15–16" compo., 1938–1940 (Princess Elizabeth) 475.00

    18–21" compo., 1941–1944 (Wendy Ann) 650.00–800.00

    10", #1141, 1991–1992 only, Portrette, blue/white gown 90.00

    21", #2195, 1959 only year this head used, authorized by Disney, blue satin brocade, net cape, gold tiara . .850.00 up

    16" #1895, same head as 21" on Elise body, authorized by Disney 600.00

    10" h.p., 1959 only, authorized by Disney, blue gown (Cissette) 375.00

    12", 1990 (see Disney under Special Events/Exclusives) 175.00

    14" plastic/vinyl, #1495, #1595, 1971–1985 (14 year production), Classic Series, gold gown (Mary Ann) . .90.00

    14", #1596, 1986–1990, Classic Series, blue gown (Mary Ann) 120.00

    14", #87010, 1996, pink and gold ball gown (Mary Ann) 125.00

    8", #14543, 1995, Brothers Grimm Series, blue with silver crown 66.00

    8", #13600, 1997, blue satin gown, spinning wheel 75.00

Slumbermate — 11–12" cloth/compo., 1940's . . . . .250.00 up

    21" compo/cloth, 1940's . . . . .475.00 up

    13" vinyl/cloth, 1951 only . . . . .125.00 up

Smarty — 12" plastic/vinyl, #1160, #1136, 1962–1963 . . . . .325.00

    1963 only, "Smarty & Baby" 375.00

    1963 only, with boy "Artie" in case with wardrobe 950.00

Smee — 8", #442, 1993, #140442, 1994, Storybook Series (Peter Pan), wears glasses 60.00

SMILEY — 20" cloth/vinyl, 1971 only (Happy) 250.00
SMOKEY TAIL — Cloth/felt, 1930's 650.00
SNOWFLAKE — 10", #1167, 1993 only, Portrette, ballerina dressed in white/gold outfit (Cissette) 90.00
SNOWFLAKE SYMPOSIUM — (see M.A.D.C. under Special Events/Exclusives)
SNOW QUEEN — 10", #1130, 1991–1992 only, Portrette, silver/white gown (Cissette) 90.00
    8", #14548, Hans Christain Andersen Series, white with gold trim 70.00
SNOW WHITE — 13" compo., 1937–1939, painted eyes (Princess Elizabeth) 475.00
    12" compo., 1939–1940 (Princess Elizabeth) 450.00
    13" compo, 1939–1940, sleep eyes (Princess Elizabeth) 475.00
    16" compo., 1939–1942 (Princess Elizabeth) 500.00
    18" compo., 1939–1940 (Princess Elizabeth) 750.00
    14–15" h.p., 1952 only (Margaret) 750.00
    18–23", 1952 only 850.00–1,050.00
    21" h.p., *rare* (Margaret) 1,200.00
    14", #1455, 1967–1977, Disney crest colors (Mary Ann) .350.00
    8" h.p., 1972–1977, Disney crest colors (Wendy Ann) 425.00
    8", #495, 1990–1992 only, Storyland Series (Wendy Ann) .75.00
    8", #14545, 1995, Brothers Grimm Series, crest colors but with red bodice, #13800, 1997 . . . . .55.00
    12", 1990 (see Disney under Special Events/Exclusives) .175.00
    14" plastic/vinyl, #1455, #1555, 1970–1985 (15 year production), Classic Series, white gown
      (Mary Ann) 150.00
        #1556, #1557, 1986–1992, ecru & gold gown, red cape (Mary Ann, Louisa) 150.00
    14", #14300, 1995, crest colors but red bodice (Louisa) 200.00
    14", #87013, 1996, Snow White's trunk set (Mary Ann) 325.00
    10", Disney crest colors, (see Disney/Special Events) 175.00
SNOW WHITE'S PRINCE — 8", #14639, 1996 . . . . .62.00
SO BIG — 22" cloth/vinyl, 1968–1975, painted eyes 225.00
SOCCER BOY — 8", #16350, sports outfit with soccer ball, 1997 . . . . .58.00
SOCCER GIRL — 8", #16341, sports outfit with soccer ball, 1997 . . . . .58.00

8" CHESHIRE CAT, 1996. Companion doll for the Texas MADC premiere.

SCARLETT O'HARA, 1940. All composition, "Wendy Ann." All original.

So Lite Baby or Toddler — 20" cloth, 1930–1940's ....375.00 up
Soldier — 14" compo., 1943–1944 (Wendy Ann) 775.00
    17" compo., 1942–1945 (Wendy Ann) 850.00
Sound of Music, large set, 1965–1970
    14", #1404, Louisa (Mary Ann) 275.00
    10", Friedrich (Smarty) 225.00
    14", #1403 Brigitta and #1405 Liesl (Mary Ann) 150.00
    10" Marta, 10" Gretl (Smarty) 175.00
    17" Maria (Elise or Polly) 300.00
    Full set of 7 dolls 1,200.00
Sound of Music, small set, 1971–1973
    12" Maria (Nancy Drew) 300.00
    8" #801 Gretl (Wendy Ann) 150.00
    8" #802 Marta, #807 Friedrich, ...225.00
    10" Brigitta (Cissette) 175.00
    10" Liesl (Cissette) 250.00
    10" Louisa (Cissette) 275.00
    Set of 7 dolls 1,200.00
Sound of Music, dressed in sailor suits & tagged, date unknown
    17" Maria (Elise or Polly) 475.00
    14" Louisa (Mary Ann) 475.00
    10" Friedrich (Smarty) 375.00
    14" Brigitta (Mary Ann) 375.00
    14" Liesl (Mary Ann) 375.00
    10" Gretl (Smarty) 350.00
    10" Marta (Smarty) 375.00
    Set of 7 dolls ....2,600.00 up

10" Showgirls, 1996. MADC Convention doll. "Cissette" face and came in pink, blue, green, lavender, white, or black feathers.

SOUND OF MUSIC, CONTINUED . . .

    12", 1965, in sailor suit (Lissy) . . . . .650.00 up

SOUND OF MUSIC — All in same oufit: red skirt, white attached blouse, black vest that ties in front with
    gold cord, *very rare* . . . . .400.00–500.00 each

SOUND OF MUSIC, REINTRODUCED 1992–1993

    8", #390, #391, 1992–1993 only, Gretl and Kurt (boy in sailor suit) 95.00

    8", #390, #392, 1992–1994, Brigitta 95.00

    8", #394, 1993 only, Friedrich dressed in green/white playsuit 85.00

    8", #393, 1993 only, Marta in sailor dress 175.00

    10", 1992–1993 only, Maria (Cissette) 125.00

    10", 1993 only, Liesl 125.00

    12", 1992 only, Maria Bride (Nancy Drew) 150.00

    10", Maria At Abbey, dressed in nun's outfit (Cissette) 1993 only 125.00

SOUTH AMERICAN — 7" compo., 1938–1943 (Tiny Betty) 275.00

    9" compo., 1939–1941 (Little Betty) 300.00

SOUTHERN BELLE OR GIRL — 8" h.p., #370, 1954 (Wendy Ann) . . . . .900.00 up

    8" h.p., #437, #410, 1956, pink or blue/white stripe gown (Wendy Ann) 1,000.00

    8" h.p., #385, 1963 only (Wendy Ann) 550.00

    12" h.p., 1963 only (Lissy) 1,300.00

    21" h.p./vinyl arms., #2155, 1965, blue gown with wide pleated hem (Jacqueline) 1,100.00

        #2170, 1967, white gown with green ribbon trim 625.00

        #2220, 1979–1981, pink with blue ribbon trim . . . . .700.00 up

    10" h.p., #1170, 1968, white gown with green ribbon through 3 rows of lace (Cissette) 450.00

        1969, white gown with 4 rows of lace, pink sash 450.00

        #1185, 1970, white gown with red ribbon sash 375.00

        #1185 (#1184 in 1973) 1971–1973, white gown with green ribbon sash 350.00

    10" (see My Doll House under Special Events/Exclusives) 150.00

SOUTHERN GIRL — 11–14" compo., 1940–1943 (Wendy Ann) 375.00–475.00

    17–21" compo., 1940–1943 (Wendy Ann) 675.00–775.00

SOUTHERN SYMPOSIUM — (see M.A.D.C. under Special Events/Exclusives)

SPANISH — 7–8" compo., 1935–1939 (Tiny Betty) 275.00

    9" compo., 1936–1940 (Litte Betty) 300.00

SPANISH BOY — 8" h.p., BK & BKW, #779, 1964–1968 (Wendy Ann) .375.00

SPANISH GIRL — 8" h.p., BKW, #795, #395, 1962–1965, three-tiered skirt (Wendy Ann) 150.00

    8" h.p., BK, #795, 1965–1972, three-tiered skirt 100.00

    8" straight leg, #0795, #595, 1973–1975, three-tiered skirt, marked "ALEX." 75.00

    8" straight leg, #595, 1976–1982, three-tiered skirt, marked "Alexander" 65.00

    8" straight leg, #595, 1983–1985, two-tiered skirt (1985 white face) 60.00

    8" straight leg, #541, 1986–1990, white with red polka dots (1986–1987 white face) 60.00

    8" straight leg, #541, 1990–1992, all red tiered skirt 60.00

    8" h.p., #110545, 1994–1995, red two-tiered polka dot gown 60.00

SPANISH MATADOR — 8", #530, 1992–1993 only, (Wendy Ann) 65.00

SPECIAL EVENTS/EXCLUSIVES — Shops and organizations are listed alphabetically.

    ABC UNLIMITED PRODUCTIONS

        WENDY LEARNS HER ABC'S — 8", 1993, wears blue jumper and beret, ABC blocks on skirt,
            wooden block stand, limit 3,200 . . . . .125.00

    BELK & LEGGETT DEPARTMENT STORES

        MISS SCARLETT — 14", 1988 . . . . .150.00

        RACHEL/RACHAEL — 8", 1989, lavender gown 75.00

        NANCY JEAN — 8", 1990, yellow/brown outfit 75.00

        FANNIE ELIZABETH — 8", 1991, limited to 3,000, floral dress with pinafore 75.00

        ANNABELLE AT CHRISTMAS — 8", 1992, limited to 3,000, plaid dress, holds Christmas cards 100.00

        CAROLINE — 8", 1993, limit 3,600 . . . . .100.00

        HOLLY — 8", 1994, green eyes, freckles, wears red top with white skirt 95.00

        ELIZABETH BELK ANGEL — 8", #79648, 1996, red velvet 85.00

BLOOMINGDALE'S DEPARTMENT STORE
   10", 1997, coral and leopard Cissette with Bloomie's big brown bag 105.00
CELIA'S DOLLS
   DAVID, THE LITTLE RABBI — 8", 1991–1992, 3,600 made – 3 hair colors 75.00
CHILD AT HEART
   EASTER BUNNY — 8", 1991, limit: 3,000 (1,500 blondes, 750 brunettes, 750 redheads) 350.00
   MY LITTLE SWEETHEART — 8", 1992, limit: 4,500 (1,000 blondes, 1,000 brunettes w/blue eyes,
      1,000 brunettes w/green eyes, 1,000 redheads w/green eyes, 500 blacks) .75.00
   TRICK AND TREAT — 8", 1993, sold in sets only
      (400 sets with red haired/green eyed "Trick" and black "Treat;"
      1,200 sets with red haired/green eyed "Trick" and brunette/brown eyed "Treat;"
      1,400 blonde/blue eyed "Trick" and red haired/brown eyed "Treat.") . . . . .150.00 set
CHRISTMAS SHOPPE
   BOY & GIRL, ALPINE — 8" twins, 1992, in Alpine Christmas outfits, limit 2,000 sets . . . . .175.00 pair
COLLECTOR UNITED (C.U.)
   YUGOSLAVIA — 8", 1987, F.A.D., limit: 625 (C.U. Show) 100.00
   TIPPI BALLERINA — 8", 1988, limit: 800 (C.U. Show) 425.00
   MISS LEIGH — 8", 1989, limit: 800 (C.U. Show) 150.00
   BRIDE — 8", 1990, F.A.D., limit: 250 (Betsy Brooks) Greenville Show .100.00
   SHEA ELF — 8", 1990, limit: 1,000 (C.U. Show) 200.00
   WITCH/HALLOWEEN — 8", 1990, F.A.D., limit: 250 (Little Jumping Joan) Greenville Show 100.00
   NASHVILLE SKATER #1, (WINTER WONDERLAND) — 8", 1991, F.A.D., limit: 200 (Black Forest) 175.00
   NASHVILLE SKIER #2, — 8", 1992, F.A.D, limit: 200 (Tommy Tittlemouse) 95.00
   NASHVILLE #3, FIRST COMES LOVE — 8", 1993, limit: 200 F.A.D. 225.00
   CAPTAIN'S CRUISE #4 — 1994, comes with trunk & wardrobe, limit: 250 . . . . .200.00
   NASHVILLE #5, "NASHVILLE GOES COUNTRY" — 8", 1995 . . . . .150.00
   NASHVILLE #6, "SUNNY" — 8", 1996, yellow raincoat, hat 175.00

FAO Schwarz, *I Love Lucy* set, 1996. Limited to 1,200 sets.

NASHVILLE #7, "MISS TENNESSEE WALTZ" — 8", long ballgown, coat 175.00
CAMEO LADY — 10", 1991, doll shop exclusive, limit: 1,000, white/black trim 125.00
RINGMASTER — 8", 1991, F.A.D., limit: 800 (Lion Tamer) (C.U. Show) 125.00
CAMELOT — 8", 1991, F.A.D. (Maid Marian) limit 400 (Columbia, SC) 125.00
FAITH — 8", 1992, limit: 800 (C.U. Show) 225.00
HOPE — 8", 1993, limit: 900, blue dress (1910 style) limit: 800 (C.U. Show) 175.00
OKTOBERFEST — 8", 1992, F.A.D. (Austria) limit: 200 . . . . .125.00
LE PETIT BOUDOIR — 10", 1993, doll shop exclusive, F.A.D. (Cissette) limit: 700 . . . . .100.00
AMERICA'S JUNIOR MISS — 8", 1994 doll shop exclusive (Wendy Ann), white two layer gown,
    medallion around neck limit: 1,200 . . . . .85.00
AMERICA'S JUNIOR MISS — 8", Fitness, 1995 . . . . .75.00
JUDGE'S INTERVIEW — 8", 1996, 500 pieces 75.00
TALENT — 8", 1996, gold tuxedo jacket, black shorts 75.00
LOVE — 8", 1994, limit: 2,400 has gold necklace and pearls on cap (Collectors United Show) 100.00
EASTER OF YESTERYEAR — 8", 1995, doll shop exclusive, comes with rabbit 75.00
DIAN — 8", 1995 C.U. Gathering, Back to the Fifties, 800 pieces 150.00
OLYMPIA — 8", 1996, C.U. Gathering 150.00
OLYMPIC BAG — 1996 . . . . .50.00
C.U. SALUTES BROADWAY — 8", #79070, 1997, burgundy theatre outfit .175.00
BLACK FUR STOLE — special C.U. event souvenir 50.00
JACKSONVILLE #1 — 8" Greta, 1996, black doll, blue sundress 175.00

DISNEY, WALT
    DISNEY WORLD AUCTION — 21" one-of-kind dolls, therefore no prices shown.
        SLEEPING BEAUTY — #1 in Series, 1989, 21", long blonde hair, in pink with rhinestones and pearls
        CHRISTINE (PHANTOM OF THE OPERA) — #2, 1990, blue/white outfit with white mask (Jacqueline)
        QUEEN ISABELLA — #3, 1991, green/gold gown, long red hair (Jacqueline)
        IT'S A GIRL — #4, 1992, comes with 8" baby in carriage (Cissy, Baby Genuis)
        EMPEROR AND NIGHTINGALE — #4, 1992, 8" winged Wendy Ann. (23" Emperor bear by Gund)
        WOMEN IN THE GARDEN — #5, 1993, four dolls (Cissette) dressed like 1867 Monet painting
        CISSY BRIDE — 1923 and 8" FLOWER GIRL and RING BEARER. #5, 1993
        ROMEO & JULIET — #6, 21" h.p., 1994, using 1950's bald nude "Maggie" dolls, rewigged, dressed
            in blue, burgundy and gold
        SIR LANCELOT DULAC — #7, 1995, 1950's doll dressed in burgandy and gold
        QUEEN GUINEVERE — #7, 1995, 1950's doll dressed in burgandy and gold
        CHESS SET — 35 dolls from 8" to 21" on a satin chess board
    ANNUAL SHOWCASE OF DOLLS
        CINDERELLA — 10", 1989, #1, blue satin gown, limit: 250 . . . . .700.00
        SNOW WHITE — 12", 1990, #2, limit: 750 (Nancy Drew) 175.00
        ALICE IN WONDERLAND/WHITE RABBIT — 10", 1991, #3, limit: 750 . . . . .400.00
        QUEEN OF HEARTS — 10", 1992, #4, limit: 500 . . . . .400.00
        TWEEDLEDUM & TWEEDLEDEE — 8", 1994, #5, wear beany hats with propellers, names on collar,
            limit: 750 . . . . .300.00 pair
        MORGAN LEFAY — 10", #797537, 1995, #6, limit: 500 . . . . .350.00
        BOBBY (BOBBIE) SOXER — 8", 1990–1991 . . . . .175.00
        SLEEPING BEAUTY — 12", 1990–1991 (Nancy Drew) 175.00
        MOUSEKETEER — 8", 1991 . . . . .125.00
        ROLLER BLADES — 8", 1992, "Throughly Modern Wendy" 95.00
        ROUND UP COWGIRL — 8", 1992, blue/white outfit 125.00
        ALICE IN WONDERLAND/JABBERWOCKY — 11–12" (Lissy) 1993, limit: 500 . . . . .350.00
        ANNETTE (FUNICELLO) — 14" porcelain portrait sculpted by Robert Tonner, 1993, limit: 400 . . . .475.00
        MONIQUE — 8", 1993, made for Disney, limit: 250, lavender with lace trim 600.00
        SNOW WHITE — 10", 1993, Disney crest colors 175.00
        BELLE — 8" h.p., gold gown, 1994 . . . . .100.00
        CINDERELLA — 14", 1994, Disney catalog, has two outfits, limit: 900 . . . . .200.00
            14", 1995, different gown, no extra outfits 200.00

21" CISSY SCARLETT. One-piece arms. This doll is not pictured in the catalogs, but is thought to be from 1961. A very rare doll.

WENDY'S FAVORITE PASTIME — 8", 1994, comes with hula hoop 75.00
SLEEPING BEAUTY — 14", 1995, waist length hair, blue gown from movie and two other outfits . .275.00
BLUE FAIRY TREE TOPPER — 10", #79545, 1995 catalog exclusive (Cissette) 150.00
SNOW WHITE — 14", 1995 . . . . .200.00
MARY POPPINS — 10", 1996, #79403 . . . . .125.00
ALICE — 14", 1996, limited to 1,500, catalog exclusive 175.00
KNAVE — 8", 1996, limited to 500, wears *2 of Spades* card 175.00
TOTO — 8", 1997, limited to 750, comes with wooden basket 175.00

DOLL & TEDDY BEAR EXPO
MADAME (ALEXANDER) OR SHADOW OF MADAME — 8", 1994, in blue, limit: 500 first year 275.00
MADAME WITH LOVE — 8", #79536, 1995, has hat with 100 on top, limit: 750 . . . . .100.00
MAGGIE'S FIRST DOLL — 8", 1996, pink cotton dress, carries cloth Alice doll 150.00
MISS ELIZA DOOLITTLE — 21", 1996, white lace dress, one-of-a-kind auction piece
JOSEPHINE BAKER — 21", black Cissy, 1996, banana costume, one-of-a-kind auction piece

DOLL FINDERS
FANTASY — 8", 1990, limit: 350 . . . . .200.00

DOLLS 'N BEARLAND
PANDORA — 8", 1991, limit: 3,600 (950 brunette, 950 redheads, 1,700 blondes) 150.00

DOLLY DEARS
BO PEEP — 1987, holds staff, black sheep wears man's hat, white sheep wears woman's hat
  (Sheep made exclusively by Dakin) 250.00
SUSANNAH CLOGGER — 8", 1992, has freckles, limit: 400 (Maggie) 325.00
JACK BE NIMBLE — 8", 1993, F.A.D., limit: 288 . . . . .125.00
PRINCESS AND THE PEA — 8", 1993 limit: 1,000 . . . . .85.00

ENCHANTED DOLL HOUSE

RICK-RACK ON PINAFORE — 8", 1980 limit: 3,000 ....300.00

EYELET PINAFORE — 8", 1981 limit: 3,423 ....325.00

BLUE OR PINK BALLERINA — 8", 1983–1985, F.A.D, blonde or brunette doll in trunk with extra clothes . .175.00

CINDERELLA & TRUNK — 14", has glass slipper, 1985 ....275.00

25TH ANNIVERSARY (THE ENCHANTED DOLL) — 10", 1988, long gown, limit: 5,000 ....175.00

BALLERINA — 8", 1989, blue tutu, limit: 360 ....150.00

VERMONT MAIDEN — 8", 1990–1992, official Vermont bicentennial doll, limit: 3,600
(800 blondes, 2,800 brunettes) 95.00

FARMER'S DAUGHTER — 8", 1991, limit: 4,000 (1,000 blondes, 1,500 redheads, 1,500 brunettes) 125.00

FARMER'S DAUGHTER — 8", 1992, "Goes To Town" (cape and basket added), limit: 1,600 ....125.00

FAO SCHWARZ

PUSSY CAT — 18", 1987, pale blue dress and bonnet 150.00

BROOKE BEDDY-BYE — 14", 1988, blonde or brunette (Mary Ann) 125.00

DAVID AND DIANE — 8", 1989, in red, white, and demin, with wooden wagon ....175.00 set

SAMANTHA — 14", 1989, white with black dots (Mary Ann) 150.00

ME & MY SCASSI — 21", 1990, dressed in all red Arnold Scassi original (Cissy) 375.00

SAILOR — 8", 1991 ....100.00

CARNAVALE DOLL — 14", 1991–1992 (Samatha) 185.00

BEDDY-BYE BROOKE — 14", 1991–1992 (Mary Ann) 125.00

BEDDY-BYE BRENDA (BROOKE'S SISTER) — 8", 1992, sold only as set with 14" doll ....200.00 set

WENDY SHOPS FAO — 8", 1993, red/white outfit, carries FAO Schwarz shopping bag 125.00

MY SECRET GARDEN — 8", trunk with wardrobe 1994 ....350.00

LITTLE HUGGUMS — 12", red dress, bib & headband, has FAO logo horse 1994 ....65.00

LITTLE WOMEN — 8", 1994, dressed in outfits from movie, limit: 500 sets (5 dolls) and
700 of each girl ....125.00 each ....750.00 set

PRINCESS TRUNK SET — 8", #79526, 1995 ....250.00

FUN WITH DICK & JANE — 8", #70509, 1995, 1,200 pieces ....175.00 set

LUCY RICARDO — 8", limited to 1,200 ....150.00

I LOVE LUCY — 8" Fred, Ethel, Lucy, and Ricky, sold as set only, limit: 1,200 ....650.00 set

THE LITTLE RASCALS — 8" Alfalfa, Darla, Spanky, Buckwheat, and dog Petey, 1996, 2,000 sets 475.00

SINGING IN THE RAIN — 8" Gene Kelly, Debbie Reynolds with lamppost, 1996, 1952 film 300.00

I DREAM OF JEANNIE — 8", harem outfit, 8", military uniform 275.00

LUCY AND ETHEL — 8", 1997, candy factory episode 185.00

THE HONEYMOONERS — 8", 1997, Ralph, Alice, Norton, Trixie, 2,000 sets 375.00

FIRST MODERN DOLL CLUB (N.Y. DOLL CLUB)

AUTUMN IN N.Y. — 10", 1991, F.A.D., red skirt, fur trim cape/hat/muff/skates, limit: 260 ....175.00

HOME SHOPPING NETWORK

BLUE ANGEL — 8", 1997, #19972, dark blue and gold dress and halo, resin wings, limit: 3000 ....175.00

HORCHOW

PAMELA PLAYS DRESS UP — 12", 1993, in trunk with wardrobe, limit: 1,250 (Lissy) 225.00

PAMELA TROUSSEAU — 12", 1994, trunk and trousseau. Limit 265 ....250.00

14" trunk set, 1995 ....250.00

MARY ANN DANCES FOR GRANDMA TRUNK SET — 14", 1996 ....275.00

I. MAGNIN

CHEERLEADER — 8", 1990, F.A.D., "5" on sweater 85.00

MISS MAGNIN — 10", 1991–1993, limit: 2,500 (Cissette) 150.00

LITTLE HUGGUMS — 12" with cradle 1992 ....125.00

LITTLE MISS MAGNIN — 8", 1992, with tea set and teddy bear, limit: 3,600 ....150.00

BON VOYAGE MISS MAGNIN — 10", 1993, navy/white gloves, has steamer trunk, limit: 2,500 ......150.00

BON VOYAGE LITTLE MISS MAGNIN — 8", sailor dress, carries teddy bear/suitcase, limit: 3,500 ....100.00

LITTLE MISS MAGNIN SUPPORTS THE ARTS — 8", 1994, pink painter smock, wears red ribbon
for AIDS Awareness 175.00

IMAGINARIUM SHOP (I. MAGNINS)

LITTLE HUGGUMS 12", 1991, special outfits, bald or wigged, 2 wig colors 50.00

JACOBSONS

  WENDY STARTS HER COLLECTION — 1994, has bear, limit: 2,400 . . . . .85.00

  LITTLE HUGGUMS — 1995 . . . . .65.00

JEAN'S DOLL SHOP

  SUELLEN — 12", 1992 F.A.D. 135.00

  WENDY WALKS HER DOG — 8", #79549, 1995, 500 pieces 75.00

LILLIAN VERNON

  CHRISTMAS DOLL — 8", #79630, 1996, green and gold holly print dress 75.00

LORD & TAYLOR

  VICTORIA — 14", 1989 . . . . .85.00

MADAME ALEXANDER DOLL CLUB (M.A.D.C.) CONVENTION DOLLS

  FAIRY GODMOTHER OUTFIT — 1983, for 8" non-Alexander designed by Judy LaManna 350.00

  BALLERINA — 8", 1984, F.A.D. limit: 360 . . . . .250.00

  HAPPY BIRTHDAY — 8", 1985, F.A.D. limit: 450 . . . . .325.00

  SCARLETT — 8", 1986, F.A.D., red instead of green ribbon, limit: 625 . . . . .225.00

  COWBOY — 8", 1987, limit: 720 . . . . .450.00

  FLAPPER — 10", 1988, F.A.D., black outfit instead of red, limit: 720 . . . . .225.00

  BRIAR ROSE — 8", 1989, uses Cissette head, limit: 804 . . . . .300.00

  RIVERBOAT QUEEN (LENA) — 8", 1990, limit: 925 . . . . .300.00

  QUEEN CHARLOTTE — 10", 1991, blue/gold outfit, limit: under 900 . . . . .350.00

  PROM QUEEN (MEMORIES) — 8", 1992, limit: 1,100 . . . . .250.00

  DRUCILLA — 14" 1992 F.A.D. (Queen) Disneyland Lottery, limit: 268 . . . . .175.00

  DIAMOND LIL (DAYS GONE BY) — 10", 1993, black gown, limit: 876 . . . . .300.00

  ANASTASIA — 14" 1993, F.A.D., available at convention, limit: 489 . . . . .225.00

  NAVAJO WOMEN — 8", 1994, comes with rug, sheep, and Hopi Kachina, limit: 835 . . . . . . .350.00

12" LISSY SOUTHERN BELLE, 1963 #1255. Blue taffeta dress, straw hat with feathers. Hard plastic. Mint and all original.

M.A.D.C. DOLLS, EXCLUSIVES, CONTINUED . . .

    FLOWERGIRL — 8", companion to 1995 souvenir doll, could be purchased separately 125.00

    FOLSOM, FRANCES — 10", 1995 convention doll, #79517 (married Grover Cleveland) 275.00

    SHOWGIRL — 10", 1996 convention doll, pink, blue, green, lavender, white feathers 300.00

        10", 1996 convention, black feather, 20 pieces 500.00

    A LITTLE BIT OF COUNTRY — 8", 1997, #79080, with guitar 250.00

M.A.D.C. DOLLS, EXCLUSIVES (AVAILABLE TO CLUB MEMBERS ONLY)

    WENDY — 8", 1989, in pink and blue, limit: 4,878 . . . . .175.00

    POLLY PIGTAILS — 8", 1990 (Maggie Mixup) limit: 4,896 . . . . .150.00

    MISS LIBERTY — 10", 1991–1992, red/white/blue gown (Cissette) 125.00

    LITTLE MISS GODEY — 8", 1992–1993 . . . . .150.00

    WENDY'S BEST FRIEND MAGGIE — 8", 1994 . . . . .125.00

    WENDY LOVES BEING BEST FRIENDS — 8", name embroidered on apron, 1994 . . . . .125.00

    WENDY LOVES THE DIONNES — 8", one-of-kind set of 5 dolls made for 1994 convention . . . . .Not Available

    ULTIMATE CISSY — 21", one-of-kind for 1996 convention . . . . .Not Available

    WENDY JOINS M.A.D.C. — 8", #79552, 1995 . . . . .175.00

    WENDY HONORS MARGARET WINSON — 8", 1996 postmistress outfit, honoring first

        M.A.D.C. president 100.00

    CISSY SHOWGIRL — 21", 1996 convention, one-of-a-kind . . . . .Not Available

    FROM THE MADAME'S SKETCHBOOK — 8", 1997, replica of 1930's Tiny Betty 75.00

M.A.D.C. SYMPOSIUM/PREMIERE

    PRE-DOLL SPECIALS (M.A.D.C. SYMPOSIUM)

        DISNEYWORLD — 1984–1985 (1984 paper doll) 60.00

        WENDY GOES TO DISNEYWORLD — #1 Sunshine Symposium, 1986, navy dress with polka dots,

            Mickey Mouse hat, pennant (costume by Dorothy Starling), limit: 100 . . . . .125.00

    SNOWFLAKE SYMPOSIUM

        1st Illinois, 1986, tagged orange taffeta/lace dress, metal pail and orange, limit: 200 . . . . .85.00

        2nd Illinois, 1987, tagged, little girl cotton print dress (costume by Mary Voigt) 75.00

        3rd Illinois, 1988, tagged, gold/white print dress, gold bodice (created by Pamela Martenec) 75.00

        4th Illinois, 1989, tagged, red velvet ice skating costume (created by Joan Dixon) 85.00

        5th Illinois, 1990, bride by Linda Bridal Shop (also Michelau Scarlett could be purchased) 70.00

    SCARLETT — 8", 1990, #6, F.A.D. (white medallion – Snowflake Symposium; red medallion –

        Premier Southern Symposium) limit: 800 . . . . .175.00

        (Medallions: Midwest – rose; Southwest – peach; Southeast – blue; Northeast – lavender; West Coast – yellow; Northwest – green)

    SPRINGTIME — 8", 1991, #7, floral dress, scalloped pinafore, straw hat, limit: 1,600 . . . . .250.00

    WINTERTIME — 8", 1992, #8, all white, fur trim and hat (six locations), limit: 1,650 . . . . .225.00

    HOMECOMING — 8", 1993, #9 car coat with color trim (8 different colors – one for each location),

        limit: 2,000 . . . . .250.00

    SETTING SAIL FOR SUMMER — 8" 1994, #10 (eight locations), limit: 2,500 . . . . .150.00

    SNOWFLAKE — 8", #79404, 1995, (6 locations) gold skater 150.00

    WENDY STARTS HER TRAVELS — 8", 1996 (3 locations), trunk set, different color checked coat

        each location 250.00

    BOBBY TAKES A PICTURE — 8", 1996, 215 pieces, California companion doll 125.00

    CHESHIRE CAT — 8", 1996, 215 pieces, Texas companion doll 200.00

    WENDY TOURS THE FACTORY — 8", 1996, New Jersey companion doll 125.00

    WENDY'S TEA PARTY — 8", 1997 (4 locations), pink organie dress, tea set 160.00

    BOO — 8", 1996, 150 pieces, ghost costume over Mother's Day doll 125.00

MADAME ALEXANDER DOLL COMPANY

    MELODY & FRIENDS — 25", 1992, limit: 1,000, designed and made by Hildegard Gunzel,

        first anniversary dolls . . . . .700.00 up, set

    COURTNEY & FRIENDS — 25" & 8", 1993, boy and girl, second anniversary, by Gunzel, limit: 1,200 . .725.00 set

    SPECIAL EVENT DOLL — 8", 1994, organza and lace in two shades of pink with special event

        printed on banner across chest, front of hair pulled back into curls 65.00

MID-YEAR SPECIALS FOR MADAME ALEXANDER DOLL COMPANY

    WELCOME HOME — 8", 1991, black or white, boy or girl, Desert Storm soldier 50.00

WENDY LOVES BEING LOVED — 8", 1992, doll and wardrobe .150.00
QUEEN ELIZABETH II — 8", 1992, 40th anniversary of coronation 150.00
MADAME — 8", 1993, same as 21" doll, dressed in pink gown 150.00
SCARLETT — 8", 1993, yellow dress, 70th Anniversary of beginning of company (1923) 100.00
SANTA OR MRS. CLAUS — 8", 1993 . . . . .75.00 each
JULIET — 8", Storyland Series, blue/maroon/gold 125.00
ROMEO — 8", Storyland Series, blue/maroon/gold 125.00
WIZARD OF OZ — 8", 1994 . . . . .75.00
DOROTHY — 8", 1994, emerald green dress 75.00
WICKED WITCH — 8", 1994, has green face 70.00

MARSHALL FIELDS
AVRIL, JANE — 10", 1989, red/black can-can outfit (tribute to T. Lautrec) (Cissette) 150.00
MADAME BUTTERFLY — 10", 1990 . . . . .125.00

METROPLEX DOLL CLUB
SPRING BREAK — 8", 1992, 2-piece halter/wrap skirt outfit, limit: 400 . . . . .250.00

MEYERS 80TH YEAR
8", "Special Event" doll with banner 1994 . . . . .75.00

MY DOLL HOUSE
SOUTHERN BELLE — 10", 1989, F.A.D., all pink gown with parasol and picture hat, limit: 2,300 . . . .150.00
QUEEN ELIZABETH I — 10", 1990, limit: 2,400 . . . . .150.00
EMPRESS ELIZABETH OF AUSTRIA — 10", 1991, white/gold trim, limit: 3,600 (Cissette) 150.00

NEIMAN-MARCUS
DOLL WITH FOUR OUTFITS IN TRUNK — 8", 1990, called "party trunk," limit: 1,044 . . . . .250.00
CAROLINE LOVES STORYLAND — 8", 1993, trunk and wardrobe 275.00
CAROLINE'S ADVENTURES — 8", 1994, trunk and costumes for USA, China, Germany, Kenya (Maggie) 250.00
ANNE SERIES — 8", 1994, trunk set, character from Lucy M. Montgomery books 275.00

NEW ENGLAND COLLECTOR SOCIETY
NOEL — 12", 1989–1991, porcelain Christmas doll, limit: 5,000 . . . . .250.00
JOY — 12", 1991, porcelain Christmas doll, limit: 5,000 . . . . .225.00

NEW YORK DOLL CLUB
AUTUMN IN NEW YORK — 10" F.A.D., limit: 260 . . . . .175.00

SAKS FIFTH AVENUE
CHRISTMAS CAROL — 8", 1993 . . . . .100.00
JOY OF CHRISTMAS — 1994, 2nd in series 100.00

SEARS-ROEBUCK
LITTLE WOMEN — 1989–1990, set of six 12" dolls (Nancy Drew) . . . . .450.00 set

SHIRLEY'S DOLL HOUSE
ANGEL FACE — 8", 1990 (Maggie Mixup) limit: 3,500 . . . . .125.00
WINTER SPORTS — 8", 1991, FAD (Tommy Snooks) limit: 975 . . . . .70.00
WENDY VISITS WORLD FAIR — 1993, 100th anniversary Chicago World's Fair, limit: 3,600 . . . . .75.00
WINTER ANGEL — 1993, has cape with hood, wings, and holds golden horn, exclusive: 1,000 . . . . . .90.00
MAYPOLE DANCE — 8", 1994, shop's 20th anniversary doll, pink organdy dress and blue pinafore,
limit: 3,000 (Wendy Ann) 75.00
GRANDMA'S DARLING — 8", 1996, #79617, yellow dress, white blanket 75.00

SHRINER'S 1ST LADIES LUNCHEON
8" boy, 1993, wears fez, jeans, shirt, vest/Texas star on back, limit: 1,800 . . . . .450.00 up

SPIEGEL'S
BETH — 10", 1990, 125th anniversary special, 1860's women .125.00
CHRISTMAS TREE TOPPER (ALSO CALLED MERRY ANGEL) — 8", 1991 .150.00
JOY NOEL — 8", 1992, tree topper angel, white satin/net with gold dots, gold lace, halo & skirt,
limit: 3,000 . . . . .125.00
MARDI GRAS — 10", 1992, elaborate costume of purple/gold/royal blue, limit: 3,000 . . . . .150.00

U.F.D.C. – UNITED FEDERATION OF DOLL CLUBS
SAILOR BOY — 8", limit: 260 . . . . .750.00
MISS UNITY — 10", 1991, limit: 310 . . . . .400.00

LITTLE EMPEROR — 8", 1992, limit: 400 ....500.00
TURN OF THE CENTURY BATHING BEAUTY — 10", 1992, U.F.D.C. Region Nine Conference,
    F.A.D. (Gibson Girl), old-fashion bathing suit, beach bag, and umbrella, limit: 300 ....275.00
COLUMBIAN 1893 SAILOR — 12", 1993 (Lissy) 250.00
SPECIAL GIRL — 23–24" cloth/compo., 1942–1946 ....500.00 up
SPIEGEL'S — (see Spiegel's under Special Events/Exclusives)
SPRING — 14", 1993, Changing Seasons, doll and four outfits 125.00
SPRINGTIME — 8" (see M.A.D.C. under Special Events/Exclusives) 250.00
SPRING BREAK — (see Metroplex Doll Club under Special Events/Exclusives) 250.00
STEPMOTHER — 8", 1997, #13820, velvet cape, satin dress 80.00
STICK PIGGY — 12", 1997, #10030, sailor outfit 85.00
STILTS — 8", #320, 1992–1993 only, clown on stilts 75.00
STRAW PIGGY — 12", 1997, #10020, plaid pants, straw hat 85.00
STORY PRINCESS — 15–18" h.p., 1954–1956 (Margaret, Cissy, Binnie) 750.00
    8" h.p., #892, 1956 only (Wendy Ann) 1,200.00
STUFFY (BOY) — h.p., 1952–1953 (Margaret) 875.00
SUELLEN — 14–17" compo., 1937–1938 (Wendy Ann) ....975.00 up
    12", 1990 only, yellow multi-tiered skirt, Scarlett Series (Nancy Drew) 75.00
    8" pink bodice, floral skirt, apron, #160645, 1994–1995 ....65.00
    Special for Jean's Doll Shop (see Special Events/Exclusives) 125.00
SUGAR DARLIN' — 14–18" cloth/vinyl, 1964 only 75.00–125.00
    24", 1964 only 150.00
    Lively, 14", 18", 24", 1964 only, knob makes head & limbs move 150.00–200.00
SUGAR PLUM FAIRIE — 10", #1147, 1992–1993 only, Portrette, lavender ballerina 100.00

**9" LITTLE BETTY SWEDISH BOY. All composition and side-painted
eyes. Tagged: Madame Alexander N.Y.U.S.A.**

SUGAR TEARS — 12" vinyl baby, 1964 only (Honeybea) 100.00
SULKY SUE — 8", #445, 1988–1990, marked "Alexander" (Wendy Ann) 75.00
SUMMER — 14", 1993, Changing Seasons, doll and four outfits 135.00
SUNBEAM — 11", 16", 19", 1951 only, newborn infant, clean and in fair condition 75.00–150.00
    16", 20", 24" cloth/vinyl, 1950, Divine-a-lite series (reg #573, 313), scowling expression 125.00
SUNBONNET SUE — 9" compo., 1937–1940 (Little Betty) 300.00
SUNFLOWER CLOWN — 40" all cloth, 1951 only, flower eyes ....850.00 up
SUNNY — 8" (see C.U. under Special Events/Exclusives)
SUPERIOR QUINTS — 8" compo. (made in Canada) unmarked..................125.00 each ....700.00 set
SUSANNAH CLOGGER — 8" (see Dolly Dears under Special Events/Exclusives) 350.00
SUSIE Q — Cloth, 1940–1942 ....650.00
    8", #14590, 1995, Toy Shelf Series, has yarn braids and pink polka dot dress with green jacket 65.00
SUZY — 12" plastic/vinyl, 1970 only (Janie) 350.00
SWAN PRINCESS — 10", #14106, 1995 only, Fairy Tales Series 85.00
SWEDEN (SWEDISH) — 8 h.p., BKW, #392, #792, 1961–1965 (Wendy Ann) 125.00
    8" h.p., BK, #792, 1965–1972 ....100.00
    8" straight leg, #0792, #592, 1973–1975, marked "Alex." 75.00
    8" straight leg, #592, #539, #521, 1976–1989, marked "Alexander" 65.00
    8", 1986, white face 55.00
    8", #580, reintroduced 1991 only 55.00
    BKW with Maggie smile face 175.00
SWEDISH — 7" compo., 1936–1940 (Tiny Betty) 275.00
    9" compo., 1937–1941 (Little Betty) 300.00
SWEET BABY — 18½"–20" cloth/latex, 1948 only 50.00–100.00
SWEET BABY — 14", 1983–1984, (Sweet Tears) 75.00
    14", reissued 1987, 1987–1993 (1991 has no bottle) (Sweet Tears) 85.00
    14", 1990–1992 only (1991 has bottle), in carrycase 125.00
    14", reintroduced 1993 only, pink stripe jumper or dress 85.00
SWEET SIXTEEN — 14", #1554, 1991–1992 only, Classic Series (Louisa) 125.00
    10", #21060, 1997, pink silk dress, lace stole 85.00
SWEET TEARS — 9" vinyl, 1965–1974 ....95.00
    9" with layette in box 1965–1973 ....175.00
    14", 1967–1974, in trunk/trousseau 200.00
    14", 1965–1974, in window box 175.00
    14", 1979, with layette 125.00
    14", 1965–1982 ....75.00
    16", 1965–1971 ....75.00
SWEET VIOLET — 18" h.p., 1951–1954 (Cissy) ....850.00 up
SWEETIE BABY — 22", 1962 only 125.00
SWEETIE WALKER — 23", 1962 only ....275.00 up
SWISS — 7" compo., 1936 (Tiny Betty) 250.00
    9" compo., 1935–1938 (Little Betty) 275.00
    10" h.p., 1962–1963 (Cissette) 875.00
SWITZERLAND — 8" h.p., BKW, #394, #794, 1961–1965 ....125.00
    8" h.p., BK, #794, 1965–1972 ....100.00
    8" h.p., straight leg, #0794, #594, 1973–1975, marked "Alex." 75.00
    8" h.p., straight leg, #594, #540, #518, 1976–1989, marked "Alexander" 65.00
    8", #546, 1986, white face 60.00
    #518, 1988–1990, costume change 60.00
    8" BKW, Maggie smile face 175.00
SYMPOSIUM (see M.A.D.C. under Special Events/Exclusives)

Please read "What is a Price Guide?" for additional information.

TAFT, HELEN — 1988, 5th set Presidents' Ladies/First Ladies Series (Louisa) 125.00
TEENY TWINKLE — 1946 only, cloth with flirty eyes 525.00
TENNIS — 8" h.p., BKW, #415, #632 (Wendy Ann) 400.00
TENNIS BOY— 8", #16331, 1997 ....58.00
TENNIS GIRL — 8", #16320, 1997 ....58.00
TEXAS — 8", #313, 1991 only, Americana 85.00
TEXAS SHRINER — (see Shriner's under Special Events/Exclusives) 450.00
THAILAND — 8" h.p., BK, #767, 1966–1972 (Wendy Ann) 100.00
    8" straight leg, #0767, #567, 1973–1975, marked "Alex." 75.00
    8" straight leg, #567, 1976–1989 (1985–1987 white face), marked "Alexander" 55.00
THANK YOU — 8", #21111, 1997, comes with a thank-you card 58.00
THERE WAS A LITTLE GIRL — 14", #24611, 1995, Nursery Rhyme Series (Mary Ann) 100.00
"THERE'S NO PLACE LIKE HOME" DOLLHOUSE — trunk set 150.00
THOMAS, MARLO — 17" plastic/vinyl, 1967 only (Polly) ....600.00 up
THREE LITTLE PIGS SET — 12", #10000, brick, straw, and stick Piggy 260.00
THREE LITTLE PIGS & WOLF — compo., 1938–1939, must be mint ....650.00 up each
THREE WISE MEN SET — 8", #19480, 1997, Nativity set 950.00
HUMBELINA & HER LADY — 8" & 21" porcelain, 1992–1993, limit: 2,500 sets 500.00
TIERNEY, GENE — 14–17" compo., 1945, must be mint (Wendy Ann) 3,300.00
TIBET — 8" h.p., #534, 1993 only 75.00
TIGER LILY — 8", #469, 1992–1993 only, Storybook Series (Peter Pan) (Wendy Ann) 90.00
TIMMY TODDLER 23" plastic/vinyl, 1960–1961 ....150.00
    30", 1960 only 250.00
TINKERBELL — 11" h.p., #1110, 1969 only, Peter Pan Series (Cissette) ....475.00 up
    8" h.p., #140467 in 1991–1993; Storyland Series in 1994, has magic wand and wings 75.00
    14", #87009, 1996 (Mary Ann) 105.00

10" TINKERBELL, 1969 only, #1110. Peter Pan Series. Hard plastic. "Cissette" face.

8" TOMMY SNOOKS, 1988–1991, #447. Straight leg non-walker. Storybook Series.

TINKLES — 8", #10400, 1995, Christmas Series 50.00

TIN WOODSMAN — 8", #432 in 1993, #140432 in 1994–1995, Storybook Series and Wizard of Oz Series 65.00

TINY BETTY — 7" compo., 1935–1942 . . . . .275.00

TINY TIM — 7" compo., 1934–1937 (Tiny Betty) 325.00
    14" compo., 1938–1940 (Wendy Ann) 625.00
    Cloth, early 1930's 700.00
    8", #18001, 1996, Dickens (Wendy Ann) 60.00

TIPPI BALLERINA — 8" (see Collectors United under Special Events/Exclusives) 425.00

TIPPY TOE — 16" cloth, 1940's 600.00

TOM SAWYER — 8" h.p., #491, 1989–1990, Storybook Series (Maggie Mixup) 85.00

TOMMY — 12" h.p., 1962 only (Lissy) 1,000.00

TOMMY BANGS — h.p., 1952 only, Little Men Series (Maggie, Margaret) 875.00

TOMMY SNOOKS — 8", #447, 1988–1991, Storybook Series 75.00

TOMMY TITTLEMOUSE — 8", #444, 1988–1991, Storybook Series (Maggie) 65.00

TOOTH FAIRY — 10" Portrette, 1994 only 85.00
    8", #10389–10391, 1995 only, Special Occasion Series, three hair colors 65.00

TONY SARG MARIONETTES see Marionettes

TOPSY-TURVY — compo. with Tiny Betty heads, 1935 only 225.00
    With Dionne Quint head, 1936 only 350.00
      CINDERELLA — #14587, 1995 only, two head, one side gown; other side dress with apron 125.00
      RED RIDING HOOD — 8", #14555, (3 way) Red Riding Hood, Grandma, Wolf 125.00
      WICKED STEPMOTHER — 8", #14640, 1996, evil witch, stepmother 160.00

TOULOUSE-LAUTREC — 21", #2250, 1986–1987 only, black/pink outfit .325.00

TOY SOLDIER — 8", #481, 1993, #140481, 1994, Storybook Series, white face, red dots on cheeks 65.00

TRAPEZE ARTIST — 10", #1133, 1990–1991, Portrette (Cissette) 100.00

TREE TOPPER — 8" (½ doll only), #850, 1992 only, red/gold dress 95.00
    8" (½ doll only), #852, 1992–1994, ANGEL LACE with multi-tiered ivory lace skirt (Wendy Ann) 95.00
    8" (½ doll only), #853, 1993–1994, red velvet/gold & green (Wendy Ann) 95.00
    10" (½ doll only), #854, 1993–1994; #54854–1995, pink Victorian (Cissette) 95.00
    8" (½ doll only), #540855, 1994; #540855–1995, all antique white (Wendy Ann) 85.00
    8", #84857, 1995–1996, YULETIDE ANGEL dressed in red and gold (Wendy Ann), #19600, 1997 . . . . .75.00
    8", #84859, 1995–1996, CHRISTMAS ANGEL dressed in white and gold (Wendy Ann) 75.00
    10", #54860, GLORIOUS ANGEL dressed in red and white, gold crown, #19590, 1997 . . . . .75.00
    10", #19610, 1997, Heavenly Angel, gold and ivory costume 95.00

TREENA BALLERINA — 15" h.p., 1952 only, must be near mint (Margaret) . . . . .700.00 up
    18–21", 1952 only . . . . .850.00 up

TRICK AND TREAT — (see Child at Heart under Special Events/Exclusives) . . . . .150.00 set

TRUMAN, BESS — 14", 1989–1990, 6th set First Ladies/Presidents' Ladies Series (Mary Ann) 125.00

TUNISIA — 8", #514, 1989 only, marked "Alexander" (Wendy Ann) 60.00

TURKEY — 8" h.p., BK, #787, 1968–1972 (Wendy Ann) 125.00
    8" straight leg, #0787, #587, 1973–1975, marked "Alex." 75.00
    8" straight leg, #587, 1976–1986 (1985–1986 white face), marked "Alexander" 65.00

TWEEDLEDUM & TWEEDLEDEE — 14" cloth, 1930–1931 . . . . .725.00 each
    (see Disney under Special Events/Exclusives) . . . . .300.00 pair

TWINKLE, TWINKLE LITTLE STAR — 8", #11630, 1997 . . . . .53.00

20'S BRIDE — #14103, 1995, Nostalgia Series 100.00

20'S TRAVELER — 10", #1139, 1991–1992 only, Portrette, M.A. signature logo on box (Cissette) 100.00

25TH ANNIVERSARY — 1982 (see Enchanted Doll House Special Events/Exclusives) 185.00

TYLER, JULIA — 1979–1981, 2nd set Presidents' Ladies/First Ladies Series (Martha) 125.00

TYROLEAN BOY & GIRL* — 8" h.p., BKW, (girl - #398, #798; boy - #399, #799), 1962–1965 (Wendy Ann) . .150.00 each
    8" h.p., BK, (girl - #798; boy - #799), 1965–1972 . . . . .100.00 each
    8" straight leg, (girl - #0798; boy - #0799), 1973, marked "ALEX." . . . . .75.00 each
    8" BKW, (Maggie Mixup) . . . . .150.00 each

* BECAME AUSTRIA IN 1974.

Please read "What is a Price Guide?" for additional information.

UGLY STEPSISTER — 10", h.p., #13340, 1997, Cinderella series 85.00
U.F.D.C. SAILOR BOY — 1990 (see Special Events/Exclusives) 750.00
U.S.A. — 8" h.p., #536, 1993–1994 (#110536) (also see Neimen-Marcus trunk set, 1994) 65.00
UNCLE SAM — 8", #10353, 1995 only (Wendy Ann) 60.00
UNITED STATES — 8" h.p., #559, straight leg, 1974–1975, marked "Alex." 75.00
    8" #559 Alex. mold, misspelled "Untied States" 95.00
    Straight leg, #559, 1976–1987 (1985–1987 white face), marked "Alexander" 65.00
    #559, #516, 1988–1992 (Maggie face) 60.00
    8", #11562, 1996, Statue of Liberty costume, #24000, 1997 . . . . .80.00
UNION OFFICER — 12", #634, 1990–1991, Scarlett Series (Nancy Drew) .85.00
    SOLDIER — 8", #634, 1991 only, Scarlett Series 125.00

VALENTINE — (see Lady Valentine & Lord Valentine)
VAN BUREN, ANGELICA — 1979–1981, 2nd set Presidents' Ladies/First Ladies Series (Louisa) 125.00
VELVET PARTY DRESS — 8", h.p., #389, 1957 only, very rare . . . . .2,000.00 up
VERMONT MAID — 8" (see Enchanted Doll House under Special Events/Exclusives) 95.00
VICTORIA — 21" compo., 1939, 1941, 1945–1946 (also see FLAVIA) (Wendy Ann) . . . . .2,000.00 up
    20" h.p., 1954 only, Me & My Shadow Series (Cissy) . . . . .1,900.00 up
    14" h.p., 1950–1951 (Margaret) 875.00
    18" h.p., 1954 only, Me & My Shadow Series, slate blue gown (Maggie) . . . . .1,500.00 up
    8" h.p., #0030C, 1954 only, matches 18" doll (Wendy Ann) . . . . .950.00 up
    14" baby, 1975–1988, 1990–1997 . . . . .95.00
    18" baby, 1966 only 75.00
    18" reintroduced, 1991–1993, 1997 . . . . .75.00–100.00
    20" baby, 1967–1989 . . . . .80.00
    20" 1986 only, in dress/jacket/bonnet 85.00
VICTORIAN — 18" h.p., 1953 only, blue taffeta/black velvet gown, Glamour Girl Series (Margaret) 1,500.00
VICTORIAN BRIDE — 10", #1148, #1118, 1992 only, Portrette 90.00
VICTORIAN BRIDE — (see DEBRA)
VICTORIAN SKATER — 10", #1155, 1993–1994, Portrette, red/gold/black outfit (Cissette) 150.00
VIETNAM — 8" h.p., #788, 1968–1969 (Wendy Ann) 275.00
    #788, 1968–1969 (Maggie Mixup) 300.00
    8", #505, reintroduced in 1990–1991, (Maggie) 70.00
VIOLET — (see Sweet Violet)
VIOLET — (Nutcracker Ballerina) 10" Portrette, 1994 only 80.00
VIOLETTA — 10", #1116, 1987–1988, all deep blue (Cissette) 65.00

Please read "What is a Price Guide?" for additional information.

W.A.A.C. (ARMY) — 14" compo., 1943–1944 (Wendy Ann) ....750.00 up
W.A.A.F. (AIR FORCE) — 14" compo., 1943–1944 (Wendy Ann) ....750.00 up
W.A.V.E. (NAVY) — 14" compo., 1943–1944 (Wendy Ann) ....750.00 up
WALTZING — 8" h.p., #476, 1955 only (Wendy Ann) ....700.00 up
WANT — 8", #18406, 1996, Dickens (see Ghost of Christmas Present) (sold as set)
WASHINGTON, MARTHA — 1976–1978, 1st set Presidents' Ladies/First Ladies Series (Martha) 250.00
WEEPING PRINCESS — 8", #11104, 1995 only, International Folk Tales (Maggie) 65.00
WELCOME HOME–DESERT STORM — 8", 1991 only, mid-year introduction, boy or girl soldier, black or white . .50.00
WENDY — 8", 1989, first doll offered to club members only (see M.A.D.C. under Special Events/Exclusives) ..175.00
WENDY (FROM PETER PAN) — 15" h.p., 1953 only (Margaret) ....550.00 up
    14" plastic/vinyl, #1415, 1969 only (Mary Ann) 275.00
    8", #466 in 1991 to 1993; #140466 in 1994; Storyland Series, pom-poms on slippers (Peter Pan) 70.00
WENDY ELF — 8", #12818, 1995, Christmas Series 65.00
WENDY SHOPS FAO — (see FAO Schwarz under Special Events/Exclusives) 125.00
WENDY LOVES BEING LOVED — 8", 1992–1993 only, doll and wardrobe 150.00
    BEING JUST LIKE MOMMY — 8", #801, 1993, has baby carriage #120801, 1994 ....100.00
    THE COUNTRY FAIR — 8", #802, 1993, has cow #120802, 1994 ....65.00
    SUMMER BOX SET — #805-1993, #120805–1994; WINTER BOX SET #120810–1994. Boxed doll and wardrobe . .90.00
    LEARNING TO SEW — 8", #120809, 1994, in wicker case 100.00
    HER FIRST DAY AT SCHOOL — 8", #120806, 1994–1995 ....65.00
    BEING PROM QUEEN — #120808, 1994 ....50.00
    HER SUNDAY BEST — 8", #120807, 1994–1995 ....75.00
    HER SUNDRESS — #120804, 1994 ....50.00
    GOES TO THE CIRCUS — 8", #12819, 1996, (Wendy Ann) 65.00
WENDY LEARNS HER ABC'S — (see ABC Unlimited Productions under Special Events/Exclusives) ...125.00
WENDY MAKES IT SPECIAL — 8", #31050, 1997, pink satin dress 80.00
WENDY SALUTES THE OLYMPICS — 8", #86005, 1996, Olympic Medal 105.00
WENDY VISITS WORLD FAIR — (see Shirley's Doll House under Special Events/Exclusives) 75.00
WENDY ANGEL — 8" h.p., #404, 1954 (Wendy Ann) ....850.00 up
WENDY ANN — 11–15" compo., 1935–1948 ....350.00–575.00
    9" compo., 1936–1940, painted eyes 325.00
    14", 1938–1939, in riding habit, molded hair or wig 400.00
    14", any year, swivel waist, molded hair or wig 425.00
    17–21" compo., 1938–1944 ....750.00–950.00
    14½–17" h.p., 1948–1949 ....725.00–850.00
    16–22" h.p., 1948–1950 ....750.00–975.00
    20" h.p., 1956 (Cissy) 600.00
    23–25" h.p., 1949 ....850.00
    8", #79516, 1995, 100th anniversary, wearing dress, coat, and bonnet, limited production 100.00
WENDY BRIDE — 14–22" compo., 1944–1945 (Wendy Ann) 325.00–500.00
    15–18" h.p., 1951 (Margaret) 600.00–875.00
    20" h.p., 1956 (Cissy) 600.00
    8" h.p., SLW, #475, 1955 (Wendy Ann) 475.00
WENDY'S DOLLHOUSE TRUNK SET — 8", #12820, 1996 ....200.00
WHITE CHRISTMAS — 10", #10105, 1995 only, Christmas Series 85.00
WHITE CHRISTMA PAIR — 10", #15380, Betty and Bob from the movie 210.00
WHITE KING — 8", h.p., #13020, 1997, white suit, cape 95.00
WHITE RABBIT — 14–17", cloth/felt, 1940's 550.00–675.00
    8", #14509, 1995, Alice In Wonderland Series 65.00
    8", #14616, 1996, white rabbit in court 62.00
WICKED STEPMOTHER — 21", #50002, 1996, limited edition 310.00
WICKED WITCH OF THE WEST — 10", #13270, 1997 ....105.00
WILSON, EDITH — 1988, 5th set Presidents' Ladies/First Ladies Series (Mary Ann) 125.00

WILSON, ELLEN — 1988, 5th set Presidents' Ladies/First Ladies Series (Louisa) .125.00
WINGED MONKEY — 8" h.p., (Maggie) #140501, 1994 only 100.00
WINNIE WALKER — 15" h.p., 1953 only (Cissy) 275.00
    18–25" 350.00–450.00
    1953–1954, in trunk/trousseau . . . . .850.00 up
WINTER — 14", 1993, Changing Seasons, doll and four outfits 150.00
WINTER FUN SKATER — 8", #10357, 1995, Christmas Series 65.00
WINTER SPORTS — 1991 (see Shirley's Doll House under Special Events/Exclusives) 70.00
WINTER WONDERLAND (NASHVILLE SKATER #1) — 1991–1992 (see Collectors United under
    Special Events/Exclusives) 175.00
WINTERTIME — (see M.A.D.C. under Special Events/Exclusives) 225.00
WITCH — 8", #322, 1992–1993, Americana Series 70.00
WITH LOVE — 8", #17003, 1996, pink gown, comes with a heart 75.00
    8", #17001, 1996, same as above except African American 75.00
WITCH/HALLOWEEN — (see Collectors United under Special Events/Exclusives) 95.00
WITHERS, JANE — 12–13½" compo., 1937, has closed mouth . . . . .1,000.00 up
    15–17", 1937–1939 . . . . .1,300.00
    17" cloth body, 1939 . . . . .1,500.00
    18–19", 1937–1939 . . . . .1,300.00
    19–20", closed mouth 1,400.00
    20–21", 1937 . . . . .1,600.00
WIZARD OF OZ — 8", mid-year special (see Alexander Doll Co. Specials & Exclusives) 75.00
1860S WOMEN — 10" h.p., 1990 (see Spiegel's under Special Events/Exclusives) (Beth) 125.00
WYNKIN — (see Dutch Lullaby)

—Y—

YOLANDA — 12", 1965 only (Brenda Starr) 395.00
YUGOSLAVIA — 8" h.p., BK, #789, 1968–1972 (Wendy Ann) 100.00
    8" straight leg, #0789, #589, 1973–1975, marked "Alex." 65.00
    8" straight leg, #589, 1976–1986 (1985–1986 white face), marked "Alexander" 55.00
    8", 1987 (see Collectors United under Special Events/Exclusives) 100.00
YULETIDE ANGEL — (see Tree Toppers)

—Z—

ZORINA BALLERINA — 17" compo., 1937–1938, extra makeup, must be mint condition (Wendy Ann) 1,900.00

14" WENDY from the Peter Pan set, 1969 only. "Mary Ann." Plastic/vinyl.

11" WENDY ANN SOLDIER, 1942–1945. All composition.